AF684081

Mission Statement

The stated purpose of this textbook is twofold. First and primarily it is to educate the aspiring Substance Abuse Counselor and related human service workers in the sequence of events called THE TREATMENT PROCESS for people suffering from the disease of addiction; secondly, to provide a basis for the certification applicant to fulfill the requirements of the certifying bodies requiring demonstration of competency in the core functions of a counselor.

 © Stanley F. Kulewicz

DEDICATION

This book is dedicated to a lady who knows me not, yet, in one profound meeting, changed the course of my being to enable me to risk all in order to serve better.

This delightful lady is Mercedes McCambridge.

 © Stanely F. Kulewicz

CONTENTS

 © Stanely F. Kulewicz

INTRODUCTION

The twelve basic core functions of counseling, though specifically defined and entitled as individual tasks, are, in reality, part of an integrated process of therapy. In performing the individual task, the counselor must be mindful of all the information gained in each of the prior steps, and his responsibility to obtain and record all possible additional information.

Information, for the counseling process, may be defined to include facts disclosed by the client, as well as inferred information gained in the intercommunication process between the counselor and the client. Inferred information is that comprehension of the client that comes to the counselor through the client's body language, refusal to respond, evasion of inquiries, interpretive evasions, and other basic transmissions made by the client.

A very large amount of information, well beyond the spoken word, is transmitted by the client in the screening process, the intake questioning, and in each of the other stages of the counseling process.

It is incumbent upon the experienced counselor to be alert and aware of the very many nuances accompanying the communication process going on between the client and the counselor. A question-and-answer technique is not usually adequate to fulfill the responsibilities of the counselor to the client.

The integration of the twelve core functions of a counselor into a cohesive, dynamic therapeutic system is essential to the long-range well-being of the client.

The purpose of the presentation is to make clear the pattern of therapeutic effort and its dependence upon that special attribute of counselors that is too rarely recognized and spoken of. This talent that sets Substance Abuse Counselors apart from most others in the field of health services is insight. Insight is that capacity to see beyond the spoken word and reach into the innermost feelings of the victims of addiction and thus help them learn a new way of life that will preclude their self-destruction through the use of chemicals.

 © Stanely F. Kulewicz

1

SCREENING

THE BIRTH OF THE COUNSELING PROCESS

The primary emotion of virtually all people seeking the help of a more knowledgeable person is fear: fear of disclosure, fear of the future, fear of change, fear of the unknown, fear of criticism, all in addition to a feeling of total loss. This unspoken state of being demands tender loving care. All the humanness that sets us apart from the animals needs to be mustered to provide comfort, assurance, and confidence for the potential client.

Fear is a human emotional characteristic with enormous power over its victim. It has the ability to immobilize and disable, or it may become a driving force to facilitate a major revolution from within.

Effective counseling techniques must, by the very nature of the profession, include the capability of utilizing what appears to be a negative characteristic by turning it into a positive force. Turning lemons into lemonade should be the counselor's stock-in-trade.

Consequently, the time of contact with the person responsible for screening becomes not only a moment of decision for the potential client but also the initial opportunity to begin the counseling process. Since all counseling is based on trust, it is paramount that the screener convey all the characteristics inherent in counseling.

Screening thus must be seen as more than a question-and-answer process. It should be viewed as the primary step in establishing a rapport with the potential client. This first step in building the bridge to a new way of life requires the utilization of trained personnel having a full comprehension of the importance of this initial phase of the counseling process.

This first, enormously critical time for the potential client is fraught with pitfalls for the screener. Lack of empathy, understanding, and warmth may turn off the potential client. It may be the first attempt to seek help. It is a frightening experience for the alcohol- or drug-afflicted person, who has an unbelievably low level of self-esteem. His/her fear of rejection, in this critical period, must be recognized as an inherent factor in seeking "a way out."

The emotional significance of this juncture in the potential client's life cannot be overstated. It must be understood to be one of the most frightening experiences an individual may face in his/her entire lifetime. A carefully trained screener is capable of providing the emotional support and guidance needed at this critical juncture.

 © Stanely F. Kulewicz

The empathetic manner in which the screener elicits the information needed to determine the appropriateness of the potential client to the treatment setting can set the theme of the counseling relationship in the treatment process.

The internationally accepted definiiton of screening is as follows:

"Screening: the process by which a client is determined appropriate and eligible for admission to a particular program. The eligibility criteria are generally determined by the focus, target population and funding requirements of the counselor's program or agency. Many of the criteria are easily ascertained. These may include the client's age, sex, place of residence, legal status, veteran status, income level, and the referral source."

The following supplemental expansion of this definition of "screening" may be used as a set of general guidelines:

"Additionally it is imperative that the counselor use appropriate diagnostic criteria to determine whether the applicant's alcohol or other drug 'use' constitutes 'abuse.' All counselors must be able to describe the criteria they use and demonstrate their competence by presenting examples of how the use of alcohol and other drugs has become dysfunctional for a particular client."

"The determination of a potential client's <u>*appropriateness*</u> *for a program requires a greater degree of judgment and skill by the counselor and is influenced by the program's environment and modality (i.e., inpatient, outpatient, residential, chemotherapy, detoxification or day care). Important factors include physical condition of the client, the psychological functioning of the client, outside supports / resources, previous treatment efforts, motivation, and the philosophy of the program."*

The foregoing definition is the standard adopted for the demonstration of competence by applicants for certification by those agencies, certification boards, licensing boards and other authorizing bodies or agencies issuing Certified Substance Abuse Counselor credentials.

Well over 75 percent of the credentialing bodies in the United States, Canada, Sweeden, as well as the United States Air Force are members, and it is rapidly becoming the standard in the profession.

The applicant for recognition as a Certified Counselor by the designated certifying or licensing body must demonstrate competency in each of the twelve core functions and its relationship to and within the entire substance abuse treatment process. The demonstration of competency is accomplished through the applicant's preparation of a written case presentation and an oral examination by a panel of three examiners. Forms and instructions will be provided by the appropriate Certification Boards.

The written case must be related to the certification being sought and should be an actual or typical case from your case files. Fictitious names must be used, and the client must no longer be in your treatment system. Appropriate measures must be taken to prevent any possibility of client identification.

 © Stanley F. Kulewicz

Failure to adequately demonstrate competence in each and every one of the core functions, as an integral part of the treatment process, can be cause for a decision to fail the applicant for certification or licensure. The applicant is eligible for reapplication in accordance with each regulating authority rules.

Competency in the area of screening must be demonstrated through response to inquiry regarding purposes of screening, process, and method of screening. Knowledge of governmental regulations affecting criteria for screening may be the subject of questioning. Knowledge of alternative agencies, facilities, or settings for referral for those applicants not meeting agency criteria must be demonstrated to the satisfaction of the examining team.

The last, too often neglected part of the screening process requires that the screener be well informed and capable of referring the applicant to a more suitable place for care and treatment in the event of unsuitability. There is a very strong moral and ethical responsibility to assist the applicant in locating an agency or service that will more readily meet the applicant's needs. This indicates a necessity for training in the referral process as is outlined in a later chapter.

It is hoped that on the basis of the established criteria above, a new set of standards and guidelines for the more effective utilization of the screening process will be developed and will result in long-range gains in the battle of addictions counseling.

The following screening or preadmission form is typical of the original information-gathering procedures used in ascertaining the suitability of the applicant to the specific treatment facility.

 © Stanley F. Kulewicz

__ EVENING PROGRAM
__ INPATIENT
__ OUTPATIENT CLINIC

NAME________________________________ TELEPHONE______________

ADDRESS____

DATE OF BIRTH__________ SEX____ RACE/ETHNIC GROUP______________

SOCIAL SECURITY #__________________ GRADE LEVEL_______________

MARITAL STATUS_____________ AGE_____ NO. OF DEPENDENTS________

NEAREST RELATIVE____________________ RELATIONSHIP_____________

ADDRESS____

TELEPHONE____________________ ANNUAL FAMILY INCOME____________

NAME OF INSURANCE COMPANY____________________________________

LEGAL STATUS____

PROBLEM SUBSTANCE_______________ SIGNIFICANT OTHER____________

AGE AT FIRST USE____

REFERRAL SOURCE_______________________________________

CLIENT IS: ACCEPTED_______ DATE FOR ADMISSION________________

REJECTED_______ REASON____

REFERRED TO ____

STAFF SIGNATURE AND TITLE____________________________________

DATE_________________

© Stanely F. Kulewicz

DETOX____________
NONDETOX__________
QUESTIONABLE_______

EVENING_______ INPATIENT_______

PREADMISSION INFORMATION

PATIENT DATA:
NAME:_________________DOB____AGE____SEX____MARITAL STATUS____
ADDRESS____
TELEPHONE_________________ PLACE OF EMPLOYMENT____________________
OCCUPATION_______________ ADDRESS OF EMPLOYMENT_________________
TELEPHONE___________ LENGTH OF EMPLOYMENT________ S.S.#__________

PROBLEM DESCRIPTION____
Current legal problems____
Family members____
Previous hospitalizations____
Physical problems____
Current medications____
REFERRAL SOURCE: Name_______________________ Telephone________________
Address____
INSURANCE DATA: Preexisting clause_______ Preadmission___________
Certificate________Advance payment/Deductible_______Benefits_________________
Primary Insurance__________Policyholder________Relationship to patient________
I.D.#_________Group #__________ To verify Insurance____________
Verification___________
BILLING DIRECTIONS____

Secondary Insurance________________Policyholder________________
Relationship to patient_________I.D.#____________Group # ______
To verify Insurance_____________ Verification___________
BILLING DIRECTIONS____

If inappropriate, referred to ___________________________________
Prescreening Interview__________________________________
Expected Admission Date:_________________Time:____________

 © Stanely F. Kulewicz

2

INTAKE

THE INTRODUCTION TO SELF-AWARENESS

The internationally acepted definition of intake is as follows:

"INTAKE: the administrative and initial procedures for admission to a program."

The following supplemental expansion of this definition of "intake" may be used as a set of general guidelines:

"The intake usually becomes an extension of the screening, when the decision to admit is formally made and documented. Much of the intake process includes completion of various forms. Typically, the client and the counselor fill out an admission or intake sheet, document the initial assessment, complete appropriate releases of information, collect financial data, sign consent for treatment, and assign the primary counselor."

Traditionally, the intake procedure has been regarded as little more than an information-gathering process wherein there is a possibility that some unknown or unrecognized bit of information or knowledge might be uncovered that could then be utilized in formulating a treatment program.

The intake stage of the counseling process was, until fairly recently, not recognized for the vast wealth of information and insight that intake makes available to the counselor. The previous practice of having a noncounselor complete the intake form has gradually been superseded by the more modern and much more effective practice of a counselor-conducted intake procedure.

The trained and experienced counselor is in an admirable position to gain an initial insight into the still fearful and ill newcomer to the treatment system. The level of attention, alertness, and interest of the counselor at this stage of the client's entry into the new experience will have a dramatic effect on the acceptability of the introduction of the new concepts.

The counselor, during this critical intake inquiry, is serving a threefold purpose. The first, but not necessarily the first in importance, is to elicit detailed, very often delicate, confidential information upon which the later stages of the therapeutic efforts will be determined. The second purpose is to establish an acceptable rapport between the client and the treatment facility's counseling and medical staff. Hostility on the part of the client will cause much unnecessary friction and delay in the treatment process. Questions incompletely answered or evaded will raise the client's level of defense and

© Stanley F. Kulewicz

serve no useful purpose for those involved. Immediate resolution of any differences must be made, if at all possible, at this juncture.

The third purpose of an adequate, complete, and compassionate intake method is often overlooked. Webster defines "elicit" as follows: "To draw out; to bring to light; to deduce by reason or argument; as, to elicit truth by discussion." By its very definition, intake, when properly implemented, will provoke thought, deep introspection, and a degree of recognition, on the part of the respondent, of the reality and severity of the situation.

Questions gently put forth, with adequate explanations, will inevitably provoke more questions about self, past, present, and future in the mind of the client. It may not be evident to the observer, but the natural function of the human mind is to follow up the spoken questioning with an internal dialogue that will go far beyond the form requirements. It becomes a thought-provoking process.

A successfully completed intake can only be accomplished by a counselor who has mastered the art of asking questions in a non-aggressive, warm and interesting manner. The ability, on the part of the counselor, to follow up an abrupt or brief answer with gentle caring stimulating inquiries will result in a greater insight into the client. The in-depth exploration of the clients responses frequently serve to encourage the clients' newly emerging self perception.

It is expected that the counselor will have helped the client to be more at ease and to begin to recognize that the staff are helpers and not adversaries. The counselor now is in a position to complete the necessary documentation for the determination of the suitability of the clients entry to the program.

Consent forms, client confidentiality rights and other required forms, to be signed by the client are to be clearly explained to the client by the counselor. It is the counselor's responsibility to make certain that the client comprehends, to the best of his/her ability, the legal forms to be signed.

When the intake has been judiciously handled, the inquirer has effectively begun the counseling process.

COUNSELORS DO NOT HEAL PEOPLE. Counselors utilize their talents in inducing, provoking, enticing, and cajoling people into using their natural instincts of survival to overcome their addiction problem.

Therefore, when a properly handled intake has been conducted, a major step in the counseling process has been made.

Conversely, if there has been no attitudinal or recognition change on the part of the respondent, the counseling process has not truly begun. It has been merely an information-gathering expedition.

It is self-evident, at this point, that information, when properly recorded, can become a source of great value in the rehabilitation process. Equally important, the

© Stanley F. Kulewicz

method of inquiry, when handled properly, should have had a therapeutic effect in and of itself. The beginning of self-healing lies in self-understanding.

Evaluation of this wealth of information, coupled with the insight of the counselor, now enables the development of the next stage in the treatment process. Proceeding in an orderly manner could very well be a unique experience in itself for the client. Disorder bordering on chaos is very often the state of affairs of the active user. Orderly transitions are more the exception than the rule, and the introduction of "process" now becomes the foundation for the development of self-discipline.

Experience, over many years of counseling, has shown that self-discipline on the part of the client has been in very short supply and has contributed mightily to the existing problem.

With the successful completion of intake, the orientation has begun. In the normal give-and-take of communication going on in the two early steps of the twelve core functions of counseling, information should have been given by the counselor to the client. A normal part of information gathering is substantiating the reasons behind the inquiries. Here again, the meshing of the functions is evident. Information taking and information giving go hand in hand in establishing the essential harmony.

The following intake forms are typically used to elicit the information needed to make an assessment and begin treatment plans.

© Stanley F. Kulewicz

DATE___________
COUNSELOR'S NAME AND TITLE____
NAME_________________________________ PHONE_________________
ADDRESS________________________________ ZIP___________ DOB__________
AGE_____ RACE_____ SS#___________ SEX_______RELIGION______________
DRIVER'S LICENSE#______________________STATE__________
IF NO LICENSE, WHY____
PRESENTING PROBLEM____
SOURCE OF REFERRAL________________WHY REFERRED_______________

HEALTH: Ht._________Wt.________Condition of Health_________________
Past/Present Illness____
Surgery____
Accidents____
What medication are you taking presently?_____________________________________

FINANCIAL: Do you own your own home?____Rent____Mtge/rent______
Own Auto_____Weekly income_______Other Income______Source______

INTERESTS: Hobbies____________________Do you read?_____
What?____
Social and Professional Organizations____
What do you do for fun?____
What are your plans for the future?_____________________________________

WORK HISTORY: Present position______________How long______
Name of company__________________________Phone_______________
How many companies have you worked for in your lifetime?___________
Longest_____Shortest__________Have you ever been fired?________________
Why?____

MILITARY: Branch_______Rank at disch.____________Type disch._______
Explain if not Honorable____

EDUCATION: Highest grade completed__________________
College attended_________________Degree(s)___________
Special training____________ Other______________________________
Are you planning to further your education?________
How?___________________________Where?______________________________
What is your goal?____________________

 © Stanely F. Kulewicz

FAMILY BACKGROUND

	NAME	AGE	OCCUPATION	ALC/DRUG USE
MOTHER	____________________	_____	_____________	____________________
FATHER	____________________	_____	_____________	____________________
SISTERS	____________________	_____	_____________	____________________
.	____________________	_____	_____________	____________________
.	____________________	_____	_____________	____________________
.	____________________	_____	_____________	____________________
BROTHERS	____________________	_____	_____________	____________________
.	____________________	_____	_____________	____________________
.	____________________	_____	_____________	____________________
.	____________________	_____	_____________	____________________

How many time have your parents been married? Mother ( ), Father ( ).

PRESENT MARITAL STATUS: (# of years)
Married( ), Divorced( ), Widowed( ), Single( ), Living with someone( ),
Engaged( ), Number of Children( ).

Spouse's name ____________________________Age_____

Alcohol/Drug Use ____

Children's names	Age	School Grade	Alcohol/drug use
____________________________	_____	_______________	___________________
____________________________	_____	_______________	___________________

Next of kin (person to be notified in the event of emergency):

NAME__________________________________ PHONE____________________________
ADDRESS ____
RELATIONSHIP____

 © Stanely F. Kulewicz

Do you believe you: Have an alcohol problem (_____)? Abuse alcohol (____)? Are an alcoholic (____)?

Do you believe you are dependent on (____),abuse (____), or are addicted to (____)drugs?

What kind of alcohol do you drink? ________________________________

What kind of drugs do you use (street or prescribed)? _________________

*At what age did you first use alcohol/ _____________drugs?___________

Have you had problems at home (____), at work (____), with police (____), socially (____), other (____)?

Have you experienced any of the following: Seizures (____), Blackouts (____), Morning use (____), Hallucinations (____), Shakes (____), D.T.'s (____), Isolative use (____),Cravings (____), Hiding (____), Changing patterns (____), Changing substances (____), Other (____) ____?

Would you describe your drinking/drugging as Daily (____), Periodic (____), Binge (____)? When did you have your last drink of alcohol (_______), use of drugs (________)?

Have you been to AA (____), NA (____), GA (____), EA (____), Alanon (____), Alateen (____), ACOA (____)?

When was the first time you attended a meeting of any of the above?________________

Have you had any periods of being totally chemically free? (____)
How long (________)? When (____________)?

List your hospitalization for alcohol, drug, or psychiatric problems:

Facility	Type	Adm/Date	D/C Date	Reason/Hospitalized

Have you ever been incarcerated? (____) When (______), Where(_________________), How long (_______). Charge_______________________________
Charge______________________Charge__________________________.

 © Stanely F. Kulewicz

*Check the substances you have used: Alcohol (___), Amphetamines (___), Methadone (___), Opiates (___), Heroin (___), Cocaine (___), Barbiturates (___), PCP(___), Inhalants (___), Hallucinogens(___), Tranquilizers (___), Marijuana (___), Others(___) ____.

Are you presently on any prescribed medications? (___)What kind? (____________)
Dosage (______________________)

Have you ever been on any prescribed medication? (___) What kind? (_____________)
Dosage (______________________)

Do you mix alcohol and drugs?(___) Have you ever speedballed? (_____)

Have you ever overdosed? (___) When? (__________) Was it accidental? (_______)
Hospitalized (________)

If you had the choice of only one drug, including alcohol, which would you choose?
(________________________________)

Are you on probation and/or parole? (___)
Name of Probation/Parole Officer (____________________________________)

Describe the reasons you use(d) alcohol and/or drugs:_________________________
____

Have you ever been involved in verbal abuse? (___)

Have you ever been involved in physical abuse? (___)

Have you ever been involved in sexual abuse? (___)

Have you ever been involved in incest? (___)

Have you ever been involved in prostitution? (___)

Are there any other pertinent data or details that you would like to add?

____
____
____
____

© Stanley F. Kulewicz

TREATMENT GOALS

Circle four (4) of the following areas you would like to improve upon:

1. Increase involvement in outside interests and activities
2. Increase social activities
3. Spend more time with my family
4. Improve communication with spouse
5. Decrease daily tension and anxiety
6. Develop greater self-worth
7. Learn to be less sensitive
8. Become more comfortable in a group
9. Modify feelings of anger and resentment
10. Learn to say what I really think and feel
11. Be a better listener
12. Appreciate the feelings of others more
13. Appreciate more how my behavior affects others
14. Gain more ability to be patient under stress
15. Learn some factual information about alcoholism/drug addiction
16. Become more trustful and candid in relationships
17. Understand and accept personal strengths and limitations
18. Deal more constructively with feelings of hostility
19. Be more self-assertive in relationships
20. Acknowledge past disappointments and failures
21. Set realistic working goals
22. Modify tendency to be too rigid and inflexible

Please complete the following sentence in your own words:
I have come to counseling because:

____

____

 © Stanely F. Kulewicz

Try to answer the following questions as they apply to you personally. Put down the first thought or feeling that comes to you. Get out of the role of husband/wife, mother/father, daughter/son, family/couple.

Answer selfishly.

Do you usually have enough sleep?	Yes	No
Do you have enough food?	Yes	No
Do you like where you live?	Yes	No
Are your sexual needs fulfilled?	Yes	No
Do you feel safe?	Yes	No
Are you capable of giving love?	Yes	No
Are you secure?	Yes	No
Do you feel you belong?	Yes	No
Do you feel you are OK?	Yes	No
Do you feel others think you are OK?	Yes	No
Do you feel you are part of anything?	Yes	No
Do you feel your life has meaning?	Yes	No
Do you often feel fearful?	Yes	No
Do you have any fun in your life?	Yes	No
Do you feel you are an honest person?	Yes	No
Do you have order in your life?	Yes	No
Do you feel you are a likable person?	Yes	No
Is there a lot in your life that you still want to do?	Yes	No
Do you feel that you are being held back from what you want to do with the rest of your life?	Yes	No
Can you, you alone, change your life?	Yes	No
Describe, in one word, how you feel right now.	______________	

© Stanely F. Kulewicz

Client #______________

FINANCIAL INTAKE FORM

DATE ___________ COUNSELOR'S NAME AND TITLE _______________________

Name_________________________________ Age_________DOB_______________

Address____

SS# ______________ Driver's License# ________________ State __________

FINANCIAL INFORMATION

Employer___________________________

Weekly take-home pay $______________

Length of time on job ______________Position ________________________________

Do you have Health Insurance?_________________________________

If yes, name and address of carrier ____

Insurance group # _____________________________

Own auto? ______, Own home? __________, Mtge/rent $___________

Number of dependents __________ Marital status ________________

Spouse employed? ___________________ Weekly take-home pay $_________

Signature of client _______________________________________

Rate per session ______________________

© Stanely F. Kulewicz

SYNTHESIS OF CLIENT INFORMATION AT INTAKE

DATA BASE (name, age, marital status, occupation, etc.):

CLIENT'S PRESENTING PROBLEM (use client's own perception):

CLIENT'S APPARENT STRENGTHS AT INTAKE:

SITUATION (as described by client):

(NOTE: USE APPROPRIATE INFORMATION FROM SYNTHESIS ON CLIENT'S TREATMENT PLAN.)

COUNSELOR'S SIGNATURE: ______________________________________

DATE: _______________

© Stanely F. Kulewicz

3

ORIENTATION

THE BEGINNINGS OF THE CHANGE PROCESS

The internationally accepted definition of orientation is as follows:

"ORIENTATION—Describing to the client:
—the general nature and goals of the program;
—the rules governing client conduct and infractions that can lead to disciplinary action or discharge from the program;
—in a nonresidential program, the hours during which services are available;
—treatment costs to be borne by the client, if any; and
—client's rights."

The following supplemental expansion of this definition of "orientation" may be used as a set of general guidelines:

"The orientation may be provided before, during and / or after the client's screening and intake. It can be conducted in an individual, group, or family context. Portions of the orientation may include other personnel for certain specific parts of the treatment, such as medication."

The orientation process is normally integrated with screening and intake, but it is very valuable to have a complete orientation session with the client in order that clarity be achieved. Misunderstandings at this point can lead to an undermining of the treatment process.

The counselor must be mindful of the history of the client's self-discipline or lack of self-discipline. Frequently the client's inability or unwillingness to function within a preset pattern of life or within prescribed guidelines becomes evident to the counselor in the screening and intake processes. The client may have difficulty in understanding the reasoning upon which the rules and regulations of the agency functions. It is important the counselor determines to what extent the client will have difficulty in adhering to the new system.

The counselor and the client are in a position to discuss and clarify any misunderstandings and resistances brought to light during the orientation session. Any unresolved issues may be a deterrent to implementing the treatment process in its

© Stanley F. Kulewicz

entirety. The counselor is in an effective position to smooth the path of transition from an out of control substance abuser to a person beginning to develop a new way of life resting on the principles of self-control and respect for others.

The demonstration of competency in the orientation function is an essential part of the counselor certification examination because of the importance of adequate assimilation of the new client into the treatment process.

An understanding of the client's past interaction with others as garnered in the screening and intake stages will provide the counselor with a basis for communication.

If a solid basis for communication has been established, a first breakthrough in removal of obstructions to change may be initiated.

The one-to-one orientation session will enable the counselor to lay to rest a wide variety of misconceptions, fears and anxieties, thereby clearing away many potential stumbling blocks. It is in this early stage of the developing counselor-client relationship that honest concern must be clearly demonstrated by the counselor. Legitimate concerns on the part of the newcomer can be brought to light and addressed only when confidence is generated. Confidence is the direct result of trust.

Questions on procedures, rules, regulations, and expectations can be fully discussed in order that a minimum of ambiguity remains. Here, again, the experienced counselor is in the best position to continue the development of the counseling process.

Since, in most cases, the treatment setting and process are a new experience, unanswered questions will inevitably lead to misunderstanding. The counselor must be ever mindful of the emotional, physical, and psychological state of the client. The use of alcohol and other drugs has had, generally, a devastating effect on the ability to absorb information on a new and radically different manner of living. The counselor, in exercising kindness, clarity and empathy, will aid in the understanding of the system and its rules and regulations.

Verbal communication must be supplemented with an adequate, explicit, and clearly understandable written guide. Many addictive persons find it very difficult to ask questions at this stage, for fear of appearing incapable of grasping and retaining information. Being able to refer to written guides limits this factor and thereby eliminates the possibility of embarrassment. Rebuilding self-esteem starts in a very rudimentary way, and its first aim is to help clients find answers without their feelings of inadequacy being compounded because of the need to repeatedly ask for the same information. The written guide giving rules, regulations, and suggestions becomes a ready reference form available at a moment of need; using it, the client can avoid the possible embarrassment that accompanies short-term memory loss.

Short-term memory loss, even though temporary, seems to accompany the period of detoxification and rehabilitation.

 © Stanley F. Kulewicz

Dr. John Wallace, in *Alcoholism, New Light on the Disease*, states that "the memory disorders in both of these alcohol-related diseases are of two types: difficulty in remembering recent (but not long ago) events, and extreme difficulty in learning new information.

"Fortunately, with complete and continuous sobriety, most recovering alcoholics will avoid these serious brain diseases entirely and will show considerable improvement in neuropsychological functioning over time."

Recognition by all staff members of the existence of this memory state of the client will contribute to the basic comfort of the newcomer. The more comfortable the client is, the easier it will be for the counselor to work toward the elimination of some of the barriers to treatment. The state of aloneness appears to be a basic barrier to successful treatment. This primary personal barrier, a feeling of aloneness, may now be addressed. Conformity seems to run counter to the addicted person's current way of life. This may well be a defensive position.

The aloneness of the addicted person is an incomparable state of being. This internal condition tells the addicted person a multitude of falsehoods. As the addiction progresses, the intensity of the feeling increases to an almost unbearable level. Thoughts of suicide are not uncommon. A feeling of self-revulsion and a feeling of utter lack of hope permeate the person's entire self-recognition.

Withdrawal from normal societal relationships often occurs despite the economic need to interact with other people. This need for interaction is an economic necessity, and as a result, the addict develops a facade or front to protect him/herself. There may be a mask that is acceptable to the rest of the world, but the internal workings of the addicted proceed on an entirely different set of beliefs.

A feeling of uniqueness, that of being different from all others, makes it very difficult for the addicted to honestly function in a normal group setting. The feeling of oneness can become the basis for the inability to function in a structured setting. This may be construed as a lack of self-discipline but may stem more from fear.

The fear of not being acceptable to others justifies the withholding of self in a group setting as well as in one-to-one relationships. The apparent inability to act comfortable and in conformity with the conventional rules and procedures of society is usually interpreted as rebelliousness. The alert counselor will be in a position to reassure the incoming client that he/she is not unique and different from all others. Orientation allows for the counselor to give to the newcomer a sense of being a part of a very special group of people, all in the same boat, trying to find a way to survive. With many addicted persons, the root cause of their anxiety is the fear of nonacceptance by members of the group. This inability to interact with others, based on a low level of self-esteem, becomes a major stumbling block in their development of acceptable human relationships.

 © Stanely F. Kulewicz

The orientation stage of the counseling process now becomes the beginning of the process of change. Change is the essential ingredient in recovery from addiction. Change comes about through recognition of the reality of one's state of being or condition, and the ultimate consequences of a continuation of the current pattern of life. At this point, a reasonably acceptable alternative is proffered.

Recognition of reality comes from acceptance of information and inspiration from outside oneself and comparing it with the current condition of self.

A reasonable alternative, when properly introduced, may then become a formative step on the road to recovery.

Becoming a part of the community of addicted persons who have a desire to stop using addictive substances requires a degree of conformity. The change from "aloneness" to being "a part of" is a very uncomfortable transition and can come about only with a degree of coercion or persuasion coupled with a high level of inspiration.

The orientation process, when handled in an understanding and educational manner by the counselor, will go a long way toward helping the client develop a new, freer way of life. Guidelines, rules, regulations, and suggestions at this stage in the recovery process set the groundwork for the client's eventual recovery through new standards of behavior, self-acceptance, and personality development.

Throughout the orientation process, as in the screening and intake functions, much information is gained by the counselor. The information gathered will be an aid in the successive core function of "assessment." The counselor who is knowledgeable in the twelve core functions and in the interrelationships of each of the functions will have already begun the process of development of the "assessment" stage.

Examples of orientation forms, a release/request-of-information form, and a confidentiality statement follow.

 © Stanely F. Kulewicz

RESPONSIBILITIES AND EXPECTATIONS OF RESIDENTS

1. To be honest about matters that relate to being a resident of the House and to attempt to understand their own addiction problems.

2. To attempt to follow the directives and advice offered by the staff.

3. To honor the confidentiality and rights of other residents and staff.

4. To be considerate and respectful of both other residents and staff.

5. To abstain from alcohol and other drugs and to take only the medications prescribed by a physician. Medications are to be kept locked in the office for safekeeping, and when medications are needed, staff on duty is to be asked to unlock them.

6. To refrain from sexual intimacy with other residents and visitors.

7. To refrain from physical violence or threats of physical violence toward any member of the community or visitors and staff.

8. To sign out when leaving the premises and to sign in when returning.

9. To be in their own rooms at ll:30 p.m.

10. To attend all scheduled activities except if excused by a staff member.

11. To participate in group therapy and community meetings.

12. To attend the evening meal at 5:30 p.m.

______________________________ ______________

Signature Date

 © Stanely F. Kulewicz

ORIENTATION OF CLIENTS TO INTERMEDIATE RX

1. Counselor on duty will be responsible for orientation.

2. Client will be assigned a bed and provided with bed linens and towels.

3. Dispensation of linens and towels will be documented and must be signed and dated by client and staff member.

4. Responsibilities of living at the House will be discussed and a copy given to new client.

5. Patient rights form, medical storage, and financial agreement, as well as House rules, will be signed and dated by client and staff member.

6. Confidentiality laws will be read and discussed, and client will sign and date form indicating that this has been done.

____

Client/Resident's signature

____

Staff signature

____

Date

© Stanely F. Kulewicz

OUTPATIENT PROGRAM RULES AND REGULATIONS

1. No alcoholic beverages or drugs of any kind are allowed in the building. All violators will be asked to leave. This rule does not apply to medication prescribed for medical illnesses.

2. Clients of the OPC will refrain from disruptive behavior.

3. Clients who are intoxicated or under the influence of any psychoactive substance will be asked to leave.

4. Clients will attempt to attend all scheduled meetings and, if unable to attend, will contact the office twenty-four (24) hours prior to appointment time.

5. Ability to pay for services is not a criterion for admission.

6. The established fee for service is due at time of service unless an agreed-upon budget plan has been established between this agency and the client.

7. All clients will receive information on all applicable Confidentiality Regulations.

8. A Treatment Plan describing the plan's length, type, and goals will be developed and signed by the client and the counselor no later than the second session.

I understand and agree to comply with the above rules of the Outpatient Program.

Client________________________________

Clinician________________________________

Date__________________________

 © Stanely F. Kulewicz

DATE COMPLETED ORIENTATION: ___________

1. I understand that my records, oral and written, will be kept in confidence. This information is governed by Federal Regulations on Confidentiality of Alcohol and Drug Abuse Patient Record 42 CFR Part 2 and any relevant State Law.

2. I understand that I am also to keep in confidence any and all information pertaining to persons in treatment.

3 I understand and agree that my success in the D.O.A. Program depends on a "90-Day Alcohol-Free" participation on my part. I also understand that detoxification may be a necessary step to achieve this goal.

4. I agree to actively participate in:

   a. _____ One-to-one counseling sessions.
   b. _____ Group counseling therapy.
   c. _____ Family counseling and/or significant-other counseling therapy.
   d. _____ A.A. meetings.
   e. _____ Hot lunch program.
   f. _____ Recreational therapy activities.
   g. _____ Vocational rehabilitation/employment assistance activities.

5. I understand that I should conduct and dress myself in a respectful manner at all times.

6. I agree to notify my counselor of any change in my address or telephone number.

7. If for any reason I am unable to keep my scheduled appointments at D.O.A., I agree to call my counselor before the scheduled activity is due to begin.

I, ______________________, understand that my failure to abide by the conditions of this voluntary contract may lead to my termination from the D.O.A., Inc., Program.

I, ______________________, have (read) (had read to me) the document explaining my rights as a client in the D.O.A. Alcohol Abuse Program, and I fully understand its contents. (These are excerpts from the Connecticut General Statutes 17-206(a) through 17-206 (k), inclusive.)

______________________________ ______________________________

Client's Signature Counselor's Signature

 © Stanely F. Kulewicz

RELEASE/REQUEST OF INFORMATION

Client's name____________________ Date of Birth_________

I, ______________________, hereby authorize: ________________
to release to: ____
the following information from my record:__________________________.
This information is needed for the purpose of:______________________.
I understand that my records are protected under the Federal Confidentiality Regulations (42 CFR part 2), published July 1, 1975, and cannot be disclosed without my written consent unless otherwise provided for in the regulations. I also understand that I may revoke this consent at any time except to the extent that action has been taken in reliance on it (e.g., probation, parole, etc.) and that in any event, this consent expires automatically as described below.

SPECIFICATION OF DATE, EVENT, OR CONDITION UPON WHICH THIS CONSENT EXPIRES:____

______________________________ ________________
(Client's signature) (Date signed)

____
(Witness/parent or guardian where applicable)

____
(Attorney's signature where applicable)
(section 2.35)

© Stanely F. Kulewicz

CONFIDENTIALITY OF ALCOHOL AND DRUG ABUSE PATIENT RECORDS

The confidentiality of alcohol and drug abuse patient records maintained by this program is protected by Federal Law and Regulations. Generally, the program may not say to a person outside the program that a patient attends the program, or disclose any information identifying a patient as an alcohol or drug abuser, UNLESS:

1. The patient consents in writing.

2. The disclosure is allowed by a court order, or

3. The disclosure is made to medical personnel in a medical emergency or to qualified personnel for research, audit, or program evaluation.

Violation of the Federal Laws and Regulations by a program is a crime. Suspected violations may be reported to appropriate authorities in accordance with Federal Regulations.

Federal Law and Regulations do not protect any information about a crime committed by a patient either at the program or against any person who works for the program or about any threat to commit such a crime.

Federal Laws and Regulations do not protect any information about suspected child abuse or neglect from being reported under State law to appropriate State or local authorities.

(See 42 U.S.C. 290dd-3 and 42 U.S.C. 33-3 for Federal Laws and 42 CFR part 2 for Federal Regulations.)

(Approval by the Office of Management and Budget under Control No. 0030-0099.)

I have read, understand, and received a copy of the above.

______________________________ ____________________

NAME DATE

(CADAC-CONF-1)

 © Stanely F. Kulewicz

4

ASSESSMENT

CHARTING THE NEW PATHWAYS

The internationally accepted definition of assessment is as follows:

"ASSESSMENT—Those procedures by which a counselor/program identifies and evaluates an individual's strengths, weaknesses, problems, and needs for the development of the treatment plan."

The following supplemental expansion of this definition of "assessment" may be used as a set of general guidelines:

"Although assessment is a continuing process, it is generally emphasized early in treatment. It usually results from a combination of focused interviews, testing, and/or record reviews.

"Many counselors use a General Systems perspective, which is analytic, synthetic, dynamic, and historic, simultaneously. Using this approach, the counselor would separately evaluate major life areas (i.e., physical health, vocational development, social adaptation, legal involvements, and psychological functioning). At the same time, the counselor assesses the extent to which alcohol or drug use has interfered with the client's functioning in each of these areas. Next, the counselor would attempt to determine the relationship of functioning between these life areas. The result of this assessment should suggest the focus for treatment."

The preceding three core functions—screening, intake and orientation—should have resulted, by this point, in much of the following:

1) The qualification of the client for the services of the facility and, to some extent, a heightening of the level of motivation for a positive change in way of life. At this stage, there should be an indication of a reasonable degree of willingness to make changes in the current pattern of living. The counselor should be aware of the level of fear of the unknown within the client.

2) Determination of the degree to which the client has been negatively affected by his/her use of substance or substances. The history, as indicated in the intake, must be augmented by the information gathered in the give-and-take communication between the newcomer and the counselor. Information above and beyond the questions of the intake form should be recorded in the clinical evaluation portion of the intake. The professional comments and initial interpretations by the counselor go

© Stanley F. Kulewicz

beyond the formal questions and answers for the prescribed form. The counselor's insight into the client, though only in the initial stage and not final, will be helpful in future assessments of progress and response.

3) A vast amount of background information—physical, economic, historical, psychological, motivational, and medical—will have begun to form a rational profile of the client. The beginnings of the development of an improvement in human relationships should have come about. The newcomer should now be able to recognize that he/she is willing to become part of the process of change.

4) The initial "probing," by the counselor, usually evokes a series of internal questions within the mind of the client with resultant reevaluation of many of the concepts that have been the guiding forces that have led him/her to this point in life. This beginning of self-recognition can be the key to the lock that can be used to open the doors for the better tomorrow being sought by the newcomer.

The aforementioned information, taken as individual facts and figures, would prove to be useless when codified by a computer. One single factor, unique to the counseling profession, is essential to complete the true picture of the individual: The experienced counselor has the wisdom to interpret the various messages as they are conveyed by the client. Not all of the communications given are what they appear to be on the surface. Statements taken by themselves as words alone can be, and often are, very misleading. The underlying content of the individual and his/her past, in addition to all the other data made available through the first three functions, must be taken into account when evaluation of statements are made.

The normal defense posture, engendered by the fear of the unknown, will color the responses of the incoming person. Subliminal messages very often run counter to the statements made or the recorded history and verbal indicators. An experienced Substance Abuse Counselor should have the capacity to recognize and interpret the whole person as compared to taking statements at face value.

Gentle inquiry, going well beyond the original question, will enable the counselor to determine those factors that will aid in the treatment process and those factors that will have a tendency to impede recovery. This evaluation can be likened to a financial balance sheet in many ways. The pluses, or assets, are determined and the negatives, or liabilities, are recognized. The intertwining of the two within the personality is the challenge that the counselor is faced with.

The counselor must, at all times, be alert to the "assumption" process. Effective counselors do not make assumptions. Assessments, evaluations, determinations, and direction must be based on adequate communication with the client. Incomplete follow-up inquiries can lead to inadequate or misinterpreted information, resulting in an ineffective assessment of the client. The second part of the "assumption" awareness is that the client has also made assumptions. These assumptions are pointed out by Gerard Egan in his book *The Skilled Helper* (page 106): "Unwarranted assumptions can underlie lifestyle decisions. For instance, Harrison learned early in life that only perfect behavior could satisfy his parents. And so, in a sense, he made a decision to do everything in life as perfectly as possible on the assumption that only perfect behavior was acceptable."

Dr. Eric Berne, founder of Transactional Analysis, refers to the three ego states within each of us as the Parent State, the Adult State, and the Child State.

The Parent State, wherein messages are implanted in our being as children, sets the pattern of self-evaluation for our lifetime. The Adult State enables us to think, to evaluate, to rationalize and analyze. The Child State, in essence, is the internal emotional response to those events around us and outside us, and to words spoken to or about us. This unobservable response to stimuli appears to direct our day-to-day outward emotional reactions.

The assumption of Gerard Egan's Harrison was erroneous, yet had far-reaching effects since the implantation, at an early age, became the basis for thought process and activity. This "perfection" assumption may have proved to be an asset as well as a liability. An awareness on the part of the counselor of this quality of the personality can be used as a tool for change.

Not all apparent liabilities are total liabilities. In the case of Harrison, an alert counselor would be able to make use of this built-in drive for perfection, in a modified way, for long-term maintenance of a substance-free state.

The challenge to the counselor is to turn such apparent "lemons" into "lemonade."

The competent counselor needs to be aware of the potential reaction of the client to various suggestions of change in life-style. This comprehension can only come about through an in-depth understanding of the client.

An adequate, effective assessment, on an ongoing basis, is directly dependent upon the skill of comprehension on the part of the counselor. An understanding of the "why" of the reactions and responses can only come about if the counselor has taken the time and made the effort to know as much as possible about his/her client's internal response system.

The detailed, comprehensive intake coupled with the compassionate probing on the part of the counselor should elicit sufficient background information for the proper initial assessment of the underlying strengths that may be tapped in order that the development of higher self-esteem can be generated by the client. At the same time, this same data base should disclose, at least in part, some of those parental influences that have had a negative impact on the person's views of self.

The generation of a reasonably comprehensive inventory of the client's strengths and weaknesses now can become the basis for the development of the individual treatment plan for the client. The strengths and weaknesses, as interpreted by the

 © Stanely F. Kulewicz

treatment planning team, will be subject to continual upgrading and change as the client progresses in the recovery process.

The counselor certification candidate should be well versed in and be prepared for competency testing in the areas of methods and techniques of assessment along with other relevant principles of practice. Verification of the client's statements and claims in the screening and intake processes are essential to the correct diagnosis of the client's need.

The assessment process is an ongoing activity and the counselor must be aware of the many unspoken changes in the client's attitudes and demeanor and be prepared to revise the treatment plan along the lines of developing need. The client, as the mind clears and becomes more realistic in viewpoints, should be made aware of the fact of the ongoing assessment change process. A clear explanation to the client of the new interpretations, goals, objectives and methods of attainment will serve to further instill trust and confidence in the counseling process.

An effective screening and intake record, along with the ongoing assessment changes, will serve to develop a dynamic treatment plan.

Examples of typical assessment forms follow.

 © Stanley F. Kulewicz

CLIENT ASSESSMENT

NAME: ______________________________________

SYNTHESIS OF INTAKE INFORMATION (Identifying data and presenting problem):

CLIENT STRENGTHS:

OBSERVATION OF CLIENT'S PERSONALITY FUNCTIONING:

SITUATIONAL FACTORS CONTRIBUTING TO CURRENT DYSFUNCTION:

© Stanely F. Kulewicz

PRIMARY COUNSELOR:________________________ DATE: ___________

CLIENT'S NAME: __________________________________

COUNSELOR'S NAME: _______________________________

OBSERVATION	ASSESSMENT	PLAN

© Stanely F. Kulewicz

5

TREATMENT PLANNING

STRATEGY FOR CHANGE

The internationally accepted definition of treatment planning is as follows:

"Process by which the counselor and the client:
—identify and rank problems needing resolution;
—establish agreed-upon immediate and long-term goals; and
—decide on treatment methods and the resources to be used."

The following expanded definition of "treatment planning" may be used as a set of general guidelines:

"The treatment contract is based on the assessment and is a product of a negotiation between the client and counselor to assure that the plan is tailored to the individual's needs. The language of the problem, goal, and strategy statements should be specific, intelligible to the client, and expressed in behavioral terms. The statement of the problem concisely elaborates on the client need identified previously. The goal statements refer specifically to the identified problem and may include one objective or a set of objectives ultimately intended to resolve or mitigate the problem. The goals must be expressed in behavioral terms in order for the client and counselor to determine progress in treatment. The plan or strategy is a specific activity that links the problem with the goal. It describes the services, who will provide them, where they will be provided, and at what frequency. Treatment planning is a dynamic process, and the contracts must be regularly reviewed and modified as appropriate."

The assessment is the basis upon which the treatment plan is formulated and is in an ever-changing state.

The treatment plan serves as a mutually agreed upon pattern of attention arrived at after in-depth communications between the client and the counselor. Without the proper input on the part of the client, the plan becomes no more than a new system of behavior being imposed upon the client. The result of such a system would be an ineffective coercion that really does no more than produce more difficulty for the client.

The curriculum and instructional resource guide *Planning Alcoholism Counseling Education* (PACE), published by the NIAAA (1982), lists (on page 23) the essential capabilities of a counselor in the treatment planning process. They are as follows:

 © Stanley F. Kulewicz

"1. Work with the client to formulate goals, objectives, and acceptable alternatives for treatment that will increase the likelihood of a positive treatment outcome.

"2. Consider a wide range of options in developing an individual treatment plan, including the components of the continuum of care, the various treatment modalities, and formal and informal support groups.

"3. Develop a complete, individualized treatment plan appropriate to client needs and resources identified in the assessment process, and acceptable to the client.

"4. Adapt treatment approaches to a client's attitudes, lifestyle, economic situation, and values, taking into account any special population with which the client is identified (e.g., age, sex, ethnic or cultural background, sexual preference, disabling factors).

"5. Assess progress toward treatment goals periodically with client and modify treatment plans as indicated."

The counselor is in a very delicate position at this moment in the treatment process. The degree of rapport and trust developed thus far will have a great bearing on the effectiveness of the treatment plan. Since the plan should be a cooperative effort with full participation of the client, any shortfall in the trust area will result in a treatment plan lacking in some very essential considerations.

The insightful recognitions by the counselor of some of the basic needs of the client may be introduced as a basis of communication for the development of a comprehensive system for addressing the problems. The introduction of conclusions or impressions drawn from prior discussions must be judiciously handled in order that the client is not offended or alarmed. The client, at this point in treatment, could be overwhelmed by an improperly handled planning session.

In the discussion of what is perceived as areas that need to be addressed, every effort must be made to be gentle and caring, since the cooperation of the client is absolutely essential for the plan to work. The problem or need, mutually agreed upon, then becomes a goal to be attained. The established goal or objective must be realistic, attainable, and concrete. Abstract objectives allow for interpretation subject to the mind of the moment and have no place in a treatment plan. The objective or goal decision must be made by the client so that the decision will be owned by the client.

In goal-setting, it is extremely important not to overwhelm the client with a number of goals that are obviously unattainable within the treatment program. Priorities, based on need and plausibility, agreed upon in a reasonable manner are in order. There is always the danger of overloading the client with all of the good intentions normally attendant in the process. The problems must be matched with the goal in a

© Stanely F. Kulewicz

simple, nonjudgmental manner. The axiom of "first things first" fits this part of the treatment process well.

In the initial treatment plan, only the basic immediate problems need be addressed as objectives. Long-range (i.e., next year) goals are totally inappropriate and will only tend to raise resistance in the client's thinking processes. In all discussions with the client, it must be kept in mind that the client has more knowledge of and a greater understanding of the problem that needs to be solved. It is unfair as well as unprofessional to discount the client's opinions and feelings. It is his or her life experience that is the basis for the need to change.

The client is usually in a "now" state of mind and is concerned with working on the problem or condition that is currently prevalent in his or her mind. The mind is constantly active, and though there may be a major shift in the client's priorities next week, it's the "now" problem that must be attended to. The treatment plan, revised periodically, allows for recognition changes and for refocusing of goals.

Since the primary function of substance abuse treatment is to remove the use of mind-altering chemicals that brought the client to the facility, goals and objectives should be directly related to the substance abuse problem. Peripheral problems that are the result of the use of chemicals are secondary, and the alert counselor will not allow the process to be sidetracked by the intrusion of a multitude of secondary problems.

All problems articulated, implied, or diagnosed are part of the treatment needs, though on a priority basis. The priority status can only be ascertained by open, fair and caring discussion between the client and the counselor. The problem should be clearly stated and the goal equally straightforward and responsive to the need.

The goal must be measurable in that there is a method of distinguishing between old behavior patterns and results and new behavior patterns and results. The measure of the old is only available for comparison if there is some record of it. This record will be found in the intake responses, the counselor's commentary, and/or the counselor's continuing notes. The client's history becomes the basis for change, in that an analysis of what has come about, how it has come about, and the ultimate results of the client's actions or inactions become the indicator of those changes that must be made to effect improvement.

When what needs to be done has been established, the next step is to determine how the changes are to be put into action.

The treatment planning team now addresses the "how" of the process. With the wide variety of treatment settings available, the decisions concerning which problem or issue can best be handled in what setting must be addressed. Problems suitable for individual counseling therapy may not be suitable in a group setting. Issues suitable for group therapy may not be appropriate for family counseling sessions. The insightful counselor will take great care in helping the client make the ultimate decision as to the setting in which a particular problem or issue will be addressed. The counselor must

 © Stanely F. Kulewicz

be fully aware of the interrelationships of the problems that exist. Cause and effect, directly and indirectly, must be ascertained and properly tracked and noted in formal records.

The resultant analysis now becomes the basis for the formulation of the original treatment plan. The treatment plan is never static. It is a dynamic process that must be revised on a continuing basis with old resolved issues or problems being replaced by newly emerging recognitions. The revisions or adaptations are usually done in a consultive manner with the treatment planning team or clinical supervisor. The most successful counselors are those who freely consult with their colleagues.

The applicant for certification must be well versed in the process of treatment planning. The ability to verbalize the following information in a clear and understandable manner is usually a requirement to be met in the examining process.

- How were the treatment plan goals and objectives arrived at, and who was involved?
- Was the principle of the treatment planning explained to the client, and if so, how was it done?
- In this case, was a change in the treatment plan needed? Why? How was it done?
- If the treatment plan was not wholly accepted by the client, what and how was it negotiated?
- Describe the procedure you used to develop an individual treatment plan for this client.

The following treatment planning forms, by their design, encourage setting priorities.

 © Stanley F. Kulewicz

TREATMENT PLAN REVIEW

CLIENT NAME CLIENT #

____

1) Substance Abuse 2) Medical 3) Legal 4) Psychosocial
5) Educational 6) Employment 7) Financial 8) Housing
9) Outside Referral 10) Other ______________________

Treatment plan to be reviewed at 30-60-90 days

Date	#	

© Stanely F. Kulewicz

Treatment Plan Review	Client Name:	Client Number:
Date of Last Review:	Date of This Review:	

1. Review each unresolved problem/goal/plan on the current Treatment Plan.
2. Use appropriate Index Number for each area reviewed.

Index No.	

Counselor's Signature Date

Client's Signature Date

© Stanely F. Kulewicz

6

COUNSELING

MOTIVATING THE CHANGE

The internationally accepted definition of counseling is as follows:

"COUNSELING: (Individual, Group and Significant Others) - The utilization of special skills to assist individuals, families, or groups in achieving objectives through:

—explorations of a problem and its ramifications;
—examination of attitudes and feelings;
—consideration of alternative solutions; and
—decision-making."

The following supplemental expansion of this definition of "counseling" may be used as a set of general guidelines:

"Counseling / Therapy is basically a relationship in which the counselor helps the client mobilize resources to resolve his / her problem and / or modify attitudes and values. The counselor must be able to demonstrate a working knowledge of at least three counseling approaches. These methods may include Reality Therapy, Behavior Therapy, Systemic Counseling, Transactional Analysis, Strategic Family Therapy, Client Centered Therapy, etc. Further, the counselor must be able to explain the rationale for using a specific approach for the particular client. For example, a behavioral approach might be suggested for clients who are resistant, manipulative, and having difficulty anticipating consequences and regulating impulses. On the other hand, a cognitive approach may be appropriate for a client who is depressed, yet insightful and articulate.

"Also, the counselor should be able to explain his / her rationale for choosing a counseling approach in an individual, group, or significant-other context. Finally, the counselor should be able to explain why a counseling approach or context changed during treatment."

The co-founder of Alcoholics Anonymous, Bill W., states on page 47 of the book *Twelves Steps and Twelve Traditions*, "We thought *conditions* drove us to drink, and when we tried to correct these conditions and found that we couldn't do so to our entire satisfaction, our drinking went way out of hand and we became alcoholics. It never occurred to us that we needed to change ourselves to meet conditions, whatever they were."

The most accepted and effective substance abuse counseling techniques, as well as all therapy methods, are based on the premise of change of oneself.

 © Stanley F. Kulewicz

The substance abuser, in his/her use of chemicals (including alcohol), attempts to modify his/her perception of reality through chemically altering the mind. The effect is temporary and destructive. The destructive effect goes well beyond the client through the changes induced in perception, personality, attitudes, and feelings. Relationships deteriorate, physical and mental health problems come about, and financial problems ensue, all creating additional pressures that are reacted to in a markedly self-destructive use of chemicals.

It is the counselor's responsibility to be the sounding board, information source, confidant, source of encouragement, promoter of hope, and a change agent in his/her contact with the client.

In the critical area of counseling, the applicant for certification must be able to respond in an effective manner and demonstrate to the satisfaction of the examining panel that he/she is competent in this core function.

The following areas must be elaborated upon in the applicant's demonstration of competence in this core function:

The applicant must be able to explain the rationale for the use of specific counseling approach used and if a change was in order, what alternative approach or approaches were utilized? The applicant should be familiar with, and able to demonstrate a working knowledge of the accepted counseling techniques such as Client-centered Therapy, Reality Therapy, Transactional Analysis, etc.

The background and the reasoning for the utilization of the specific treatment program or combinations such as group, individual, family, in-patient, out-patient, partial program, etc., needs to be clearly explained to the inquiring panel. The applicant needs to be able to indicate the client's changes and growth in relation to the treatment plan and subsequent treatment plan changes. Provision of information as to the methods used to foster the client's ability to recognize problems and determine paths of solution to the problems must be clearly explained.

A detailed explanation of the methods used to help the client recognize, define and verbalize emotions within the client's cultural, gender and individual backgrounds will demonstrate the counselor applicants counseling ability.

Carl Rogers and C. B. Truax in *The Therapeutic Relationship and Its Impact* (1967) state:

"In relation to therapy, CONGRUENCE means that the therapist is what he is, during the encounter with the client. He is without front or facade, openly being the feelings and attitudes which at the moment are flowing in him. It involves the element of self-awareness, meaning that the feelings the therapist is experiencing are available to him, available to his awareness, and also that he is able to live these feeling, to be them in the relationship, and be able to communicate them if appropriate. It means that he comes into direct personal encounter with his client, meeting him on a person-to-person basis. It means that he is being himself, not denying himself."

 © Stanley F. Kulewicz

The resultant genuineness allows the counselor to be spontaneous, thereby engendering spontaneity in the client. Such an attitude on the part of the counselor results in a consistency of honesty that tends to inspire the client to respond in an honest and forthright manner.

The counselor's task is to motivate the client to make positive changes. These positive changes are changes of perception of self, viewpoints of responsibility, willingness to accept responsibility for self, and a host of other very important changes. The counselor can make no changes in his/her client. The counselor becomes the catalyst in the treatment environment, providing space, time, and support for the client to seek out the best possible manner of changing self.

Jess Lair, Ph.D., in his book *I ain't much, baby—but I'm all I've got*, states, "The idea of acceptance has been around two thousand years. It's the heart of Alcoholics Anonymous and Emotions Anonymous. The best expression that I've seen of this idea is by Carl Rogers. He says, 'The curious paradox is that when I accept myself just as I am, then I can change.' "

Since there is no one, single counseling approach to meet the varied needs of the many clients counselors work with, it is essential that a working knowledge of a multitude of counseling techniques be a part of their therapeutic kit. The utilization of a variety of techniques usually results in the counselor's developing an eclectic system of his/her own that will fit the needs of the clients.

In order that appropriate changes in technique can be made, there must be a written basis of information. The counselor's progress notes—providing for information gathered in the counseling session, an assessment or evaluation of the data, and a plan to resolve issues raised or for planned direction—are an essential ingredient in the treatment process.

The magnitude of the data or information varies with the agency's requirements or the counselor's needs. An important factor in counselor's notes is that they must, for the client's well-being, be extensive enough for a replacement counselor to continue the process without undue stress on the client. The replacement counselor should not be forced to reconstruct the entire case due to faulty or inadequate clinician's notes.

Counselor's progress notes are an essential part of the case conference process as well as the basis for the consideration of treatment planning changes. Additionally, progress notes are an invaluable tool in working with significant others in family counseling. Judicious use of counselor progress notes can be a very valuable source of basic family interaction information for the development of the family counseling process. Family counseling can be the beginning of the development of a support system outside of, but working with, the immediate treatment process.

Without effective counselor's progress notes, the development and implementation of a useful discharge plan and after-care program may fail to meet the continuing needs of the client, and he/she will not have been well served.

Examples of progress note forms follow.

 © Stanely F. Kulewicz

PROGRESS NOTES

DATE:	CLIENT: COUNSELOR:

 © Stanely F. Kulewicz

Client Name

Date	Observation (Data)	Assessment	Plan
#1			
			COUNSELOR SIGNATURE
#2			
			COUNSELOR SIGNATURE
#3			
			COUNSELOR SIGNATURE
#4			
			COUNSELOR SIGNATURE

© Stanely F. Kulewicz

7

CASE MANAGEMENT

THE TEAM AT WORK

The internationally accepted definition of case management is as follows:

"CASE MANAGEMENT—Activities which bring services, agencies, resources, or people together within a planned framework of action toward the achievement of established goals. It may involve liaison activities and collateral contacts."

The following supplemental expansion of this definition of "case management" may be used as a set of general guidelines:

"Case Management is the coordination of a multiple-service plan. By the time many alcohol and other drug abusers enter treatment, they tend to manifest dysfunctioning in a variety of areas. For example, a heroin addict may have hepatitis, lack job skills, and have a pending criminal charge. In this case, the counselor might monitor his medical treatment, make a referral to a vocational rehabilitation program, and communicate with representatives of the criminal justice system.

"The client may also be receiving other treatment services, such as family therapy and chemotherapy, within the same agency. These activities must be integrated into the treatment plan, and communication must be maintained with the appropriate personnel."

In the treatment process, either inpatient or outpatient, the basic concepts remain the same. Effective treatment is contingent upon a cooperative effort of the client and the treatment staff. The treatment staff usually consists of the primary counselor, clinical supervisor, staff psychologist, and consulting psychiatrist. It is not unusual to include the staff physician and/or nursing staff member in those cases where it is appropriate to meet the individual client's needs. The interacting and consulting efforts on the part of the team enable the treatment process to be continually monitored and updated on an ongoing, regular basis.

Scheduled case management staff meetings should be on a frequent enough basis to allow for a reasonably current review of the case. Since counselors require a reasonable degree of latitude in their counseling efforts, case management meetings should allow adequate time, between reviews, to allow for demonstration of results of possible changes in the counselor's approach. Since the counselor's approach or technique may have to be changed on the basis of immediate need, the counselor on the

 © Stanley F. Kulewicz

firing line should feel unencumbered by the idea of *second-guessing* on the part of the remainder of the team.

In those instances when there may be a need to consult immediately, the Clinical Supervisor should be readily available for discussion to meet the need.

Counselor's progress notes are the essential ingredient in the case management process. Adequate records of prior counseling sessions and/or observations constitute the basis for discussion of each case. Properly recorded, this information base, containing both objective and subjective information, will support the counselor in his/her views and thereby provide a reasonable discussion base for the case management team.

The clinician's notes should reflect adequate information as to the happenings and discussions during the case management conference to enable the counselor to review the experience and revise his/her plans or counseling techniques. The case conference allows for the verbalization of the counselor's feelings about the progress of the subject client. This process of putting into the spoken word the impressions and feelings about the client has the effect of clarifying and organizing the counselor's internal processes.

Until the thoughts and impressions are spoken, they are merely theories and of limited substance. When spoken and clarified, they become substantial and can be shared with the case management team for discussion and development. The resulting feedback will provide a basis for possible revision of the treatment plan.

The PACE Manual (page 148) states: "... the problems of alcoholism [drug abuse] clients are often multiple [and] complex, and require simultaneous involvement of more than one helping profession in more than one agency. These various services must be coordinated and monitored to ensure continuity of care. The alcoholism [drug abuse] counselor may be coordinator of the treatment [case management] team or may be a member of the team." The case management team usually formulates the selection and introduction of additional services when required.

The interrelationship of treatment planning and case management is indicative of the entire 12 core function integration in the treatment process.

The case management conference frequently uncovers and develops a need for contact with other agencies or services not yet addressed. When the need arises for contact with other agencies or services outside the immediate treatment facility, proper release and request-for-information forms must be signed.

Authorization for a disclosure consent form is mandatory. The proper forms must be filled in completely and signed and witnessed. It is incumbent upon the counselor to explain to the client, in detail, the purpose of the request for transfer of information.

 © Stanely F. Kulewicz

Since the success of the treatment process depends on the cooperation of the client, any failure to advise and educate the client will impede the process.

It is advisable in most cases to provide copies of signed forms to the client. This information process will aid in the development of a higher level of trust. When there is no ambiguity or question as to the purpose of any of the procedures, a higher level of confidence in the counselor and the staff is more likely to develop. Full information, freely given to the client, can be a major factor in redeveloping trust in others. The therapeutic effect of this mutual disclosure cannot be measured on an objective level but will manifest itself in improved interaction between the client and the counselor.

The counselor certification candidate must be well versed in the processes, protocols and procedures of each member of the case management team. A broad based understanding of each case management team member's function, limitations and resources will serve the counselor well in the development and advancement of the client's well being. The paramount source of basic information and initial interpretation of client actions, reactions and responsiveness lies with the primary counselor. All pertinent knowledge of the client must be readily available to the counselor in the case conference. The counselor's progress notes serve as the basis for discussion and analysis with the other team members participation.

The certification candidate must be able to demonstrate competence through relating and interpreting the client's response to counseling techniques utilized. The candidate should be able to explain his/her rationale for any change in counseling approaches along with relevant information on the involvement of other personnel in the case management part of the treatment process.

Information on contact and/or utilization of agencies or services outside the counselor's agency is an area that the candidate must be able to provide. Reference should be made to all relevant forms required for disclosure of information while demonstrating competence in the core function of case management.

The following forms cover Principles of Confidentiality for Alcohol and Drug Abuse Treatment Records; Confidentiality of Alcohol and Drug Abuse Patient Records; Consent for the Release of Confidential Information; Authorization for Release of Medical Information; and Authorization of Disclosures Notification Consent Form.

 © Stanley F. Kulewicz

PRINCIPLES OF CONFIDENTIALITY FOR ALCOHOL AND DRUG ABUSE TREATMENT RECORDS

1) Federal Regulations take precedence over State Statute unless the latter is stronger.

2) Federal Regulations allow disclosure of patient identifying information only under the following circumstances:

   A) When the patient has consented in writing:

      i) consent must be in the form required by Federal Regulations.
      ii) written notice to the recipient prohibiting redisclosure of the information must accompany the disclosure.

   B) When there is a medical emergency regarding a specific patient.

   C) When a patient commits or threatens to commit a crime on the premises of the program or against program personnel:

      i) report to the police can't identify person as a patient.

   D) To qualified personnel conducting scientific research, management or financial audits, or program evaluation:

      i) redisclosure of patient identifying information by researcher is prohibited.

   E) When it is required by a court order:

      i) a subpoena is not adequate and a hearing must be held before a court order can be issued.
      ii) disclosure is limited to objective data, i.e., dates of enrollment and discharge, attendance, medication, lab reports, etc.

NOTE THAT B, C, D AND E DO NOT REQUIRE PATIENT CONSENT!

3) If a request for patient identifying information does not fall within the five items listed above,

   i) the information may not be disclosed, and
   ii) your response must be noncommittal. If you are not sure, do not give out any information.

PATIENT IDENTIFYING INFORMATION INCLUDES EVEN THE NAME OF A CURRENT, FORMER, OR DECEASED PATIENT.

© Stanely F. Kulewicz

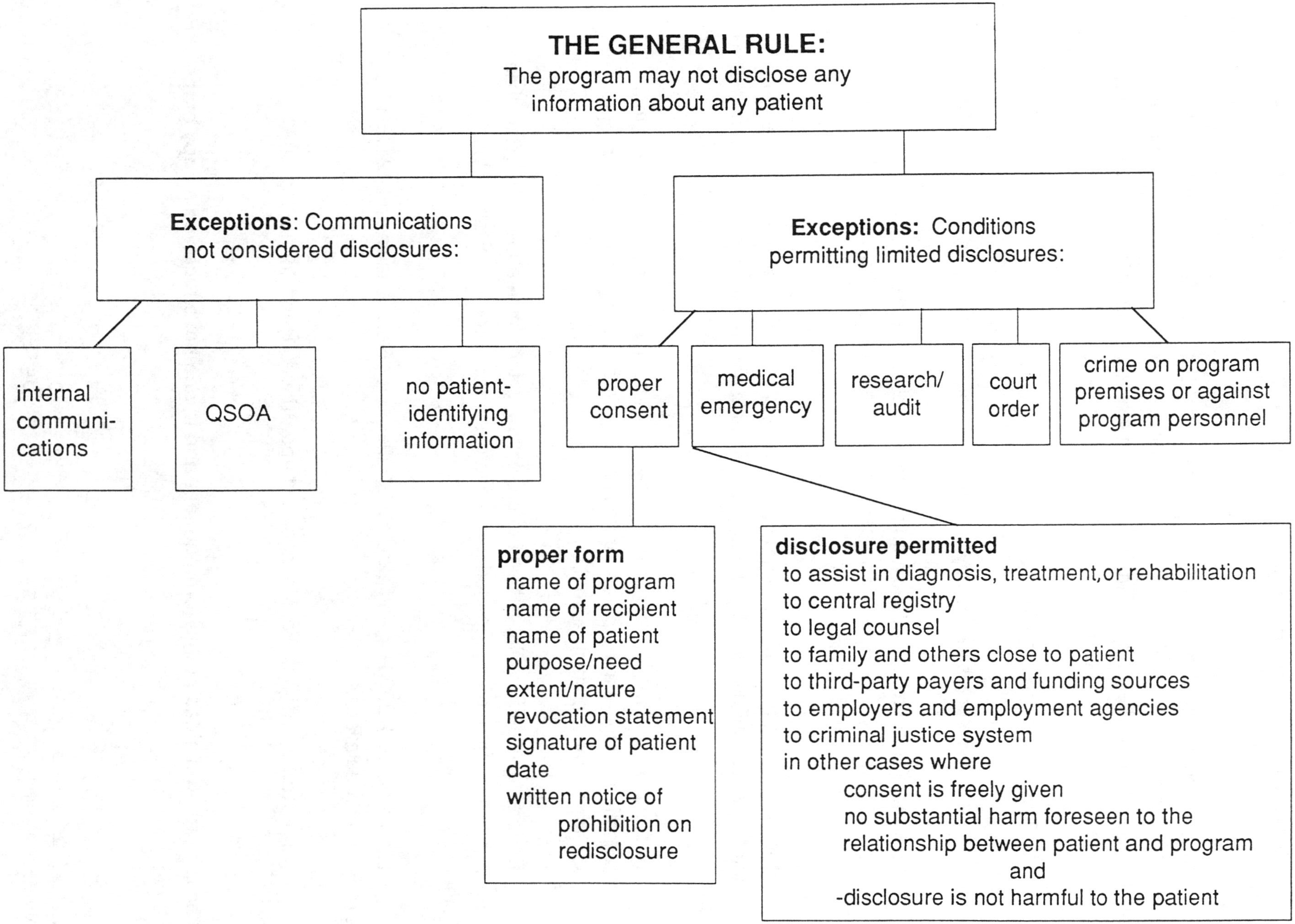

© Stanely F. Kulewicz

CONFIDENTIALITY OF ALCOHOL AND DRUG ABUSE PATIENT RECORDS

The confidentiality of alcohol and drug abuse patient records maintained by this program is protected by Federal law and regulations. Generally, the program may not say to a person outside the program that a patient attends the program, or disclose any information identifying a patient as an alcohol or drug abuser unless:

(1) The patient consents in writing;

(2) The disclosure is allowed by a court order; or

(3) The disclosure is made to medical personnel in a medical emergency or to qualified personnel for research, audit, or program evaluation.

Violation of the Federal law and regulations by a program is a crime. Suspected violations may be reported to appropriate authorities in accordance with Federal regulations.

Federal law and regulations do not protect any information about a crime committed by a patient either at the program or against any person who works for the program or about any threat to commit such a crime.

Federal laws and regulations do not protect any information about suspected child abuse or neglect from being reported under State law to appropriate State or local authorities.

(See 42 U.S.C. 290dd-3 and 42 U.S.C. 290ee-3 for Federal laws and 42 CFR Part 2 of Federal regulations.)

(Approved by the Office of Management and Budget under Control No. 0030-0099.)

I have read both sides of this form, understand it, and have received a copy of the above.

______________________________ ______________

NAME DATE

© Stanely F. Kulewicz

CONSENT FOR THE RELEASE OF CONFIDENTIAL INFORMATION

1. I,.________________________________, AUTHORIZE THE FOLLOWING DISCLOSURE OF INFORMATION FROM MY TREATMENT RECORD:

2. NAME OF PROGRAM THAT IS TO MAKE THE DISCLOSURE:___________
____

3. NAME OR TITLE OF PERSON OR ORGANIZATION TO WHICH THE DISCLOSURE IS TO BE MADE: ______________________________
____

4. PURPOSE OR NEED OF DISCLOSURE: _________________________
____

5. EXTENT OR NATURE OF INFORMATION TO BE DISCLOSED: ___________
____

6. DATE OF BIRTH: ____

7. THIS CONSENT IS SUBJECT TO REVOCATION AT ANY TIME EXCEPT TO THE EXTENT THAT ACTION HAS BEEN TAKEN IN RELIANCE THEREON. IF NOT PREVIOUSLY REVOKED, THIS CONSENT WILL TERMINATE UPON (SPECIFIC DATE, EVENT, OR CONDITION):
____

8. SIGNATURE OF PATIENT:______________________________________

   SIGNATURE OF PARENT OR GUARDIAN: __________________________

   SIGNATURE OF PERSON AUTHORIZED TO SIGN IN LIEU OF THE PATIENT (WHERE REQUIRED): ____________________________________

9. DATE ON WHICH THIS CONSENT IS SIGNED: ______________________

I understand that my records are protected under the Federal and State confidentiality Regulations and cannot be disclosed without my written consent unless otherwise provided for in the regulations. I also understand that I may revoke this consent at any time except to the extent that action has been taken in reliance on it (e.g., probation or parole) and that in any event this consent expires automatically as described above.

© Stanely F. Kulewicz

AUTHORIZATION FOR RELEASE OF MEDICAL INFORMATION

INFORMATION HOLDER AND ADDRESS:

CLIENT'S FULL NAME:

I hereby request and authorize the above-named information holder to release to this treatment facility appropriate Medical/Psychiatric information pertaining to me and this appointment. This information is released for purposes associated with my residence and treatment at this facility, a residential alcohol rehabilitation agency. Attending physician, please use this space for appropriate information, including diagnosis, recommendation, and medication prescribed.

This authorization may be revoked by me at any time, except to the extent that action has been taken in reliance thereon. This authorization, unless expressly revoked earlier, expires upon ______________________________.

Date

Signed____________________________________ Date_______________

Witness___________________________________ Date_______________

 © Stanely F. Kulewicz

AUTHORIZATION OF DISCLOSURES NOTIFICATION CONSENT FORM

I, ______________________________________,

authorize ___________________________________ to notify and inform

____

____

____

____

of my presence in the facility.

In addition, I authorize the acknowledgment of my presence in this facility to callers and visitors.

The purpose of the disclosure authorized herein is to provide information to parties personally interested in my whereabouts.

This consent may be revoked by me at any time except to the extent that action has been taken in reliance thereon. This consent (unless expressly revoked earlier) expires upon my formal discharge from this facility.

____

Signature of client-patient DATE

____

Signature of witness DATE

____

Signature of parent, guardian, or legal representative DATE

____

Specify relationship

 © Stanely F. Kulewicz

8

CRISIS INTERVENTION

LEMONS INTO LEMONADE

The internationally accepted definition of crisis intervention is as follows:

"CRISIS INTERVENTION—Those services which respond to an alcohol and / or other drug abuser's needs during acute emotional and / or physical distress."

The following supplemental expansion of this definition of "crisis intervention" may be used as a set of general guidelines:

"A crisis is a decisive, crucial event in the course of treatment that threatens to compromise or destroy the rehabilitation effort. These crises may be directly related to alcohol and or drug use (i.e., overdose or relapse) or indirectly related. The latter might include the death of a significant other, separation / divorce, arrest, suicidal gestures, psychotic episode, or outside pressure to terminate treatment.

"It is imperative that the counselor be able to mitigate or resolve the immediate problem and use the negative events to enhance the treatment effort, if possible."

Since each crisis is of limited duration, the resolution of the crisis may come about at any stage of its development. Much of this development lies within a client's thought processes. The alert and resourceful counselor will note client changes in attitude or concentration preceding overt crisis indicators.

If there is a prospect of the client's leaving the treatment center, an analysis of the attitudinal changes may indicate that there are outside forces working in the situation that need to be addressed. These forces may include pressure from significant others to leave treatment, economic pressures, cultural factors, or denial.

In the event of pressure from significant others to leave treatment, a conference of all the participants with the counselor may resolve the issue. There may be doubts and questions on the part of the significant others that have been contributing to the problem. Adequate information could provide a basis for a change in their viewpoint.

If cultural factors are having a negative influence upon the treatment process and are creating a crisis, consultation with a knowledgeable consultant may provide the basis for solving the crisis.

The applicant for certification must be prepared to demonstrate competency, to

 © Stanley F. Kulewicz

the satisfaction of the examiners, in handling a wide range of potential crisis situations. It is important that the applicant be able to define a crisis and to give an example and other pertinent information in the case, such as how the crisis was handled and how it was used to enhance the client's treatment. Questions may be asked in the area of a client having HIV positive results and the handling of this problem in the agency. Questions may also be asked in the area of actions taken or not taken in the event of psychotic episodes on the part of the client.

In demonstrating competence in this core function, the counselor candidate must convey a good working knowledge of the definition of a crisis. The competent counselor will constantly be alert to the potential situations that might arise to put the treatment process gains in jeopardy. A crisis in being should be turned into a treatment asset enhancing the treatment process by helping the client develop his/her abilities to cope with the situation without the escape of chemicals. The counselor's recognition of an imminent crisis opens the door to dialogue to short circuit the impending problems.

The development of a trustful client-counselor relationship, with in-depth communication, puts the counselor in a position to discern a potential crisis in the client's near future. With an appropriate working relationship with the client, the counselor might be able to prepare the client for the impending crisis and thereby minimize its negative effect.

To the counselor, a crisis is a golden opportunity to utilize his/her skills in changing the end result of the crisis. The alert counselor, if adequately prepared, should be able to relate the current crisis to a past experience of the client and turn the apparently negative current situation into a positive force. A complete record and an in-depth understanding of the client are essential to the positive utilization of the current crisis. Comprehensive progress notes, coupled with the complete intake information, frequently provides clues to the pattern of the client's reactions in crisis situations.

The degree of immediacy with which the emerging crisis is handled is crucial to a successful treatment process. The crisis may have been in a developing stage with concomitant attitudinal changes in the client. The alert counselor should be able to pick up on the client's changing demeanor and probe to define the developing disturbance. Crisis prevention should be in the forefront of the counselor's agenda. This requires a high degree of insight on the part of the counselor and is an essential skill in the profession. Crisis prevention, when possible, is preferable to crisis resolution.

Terence T. Gorski, in his book *Counseling for Relapse Prevention*, has developed a chart of indicators that precede the act of using. Gorski's chart follows this chapter. Gorski defines relapse as follows: "Relapse is a process that occurs within the patient which manifests itself in a progressive pattern of behavior that allows the symptoms of a disease or illness to become reactivated in a person who has previously arrested those symptoms."

The current event that appears to have precipitated the crisis frequently has its

© Stanley F. Kulewicz

roots in the perceptions and attitudes of the client. Since these are in a state of continual flux, the counselor should be alert to attitudinal changes that would indicate a change in the internal processing of information and impressions by the client. The incident that has precipitated the crisis is frequently the aftermath of negative and self-defeating thinking. A low level of self-worth tends to magnify the enormity of the immediate incident.

The counseling process should include a major effort to reinforce the client's ability to take life on life's terms with all of the negative and positive incidents on a daily basis. A major effort must be made in the area of viewing incidents and conditions in light of the entire being of the client. The tendency of the substance abuser is to overreact to an unexpected or unacceptable occurrence by reverting to his/her regular coping mechanism.

The *PACE Curriculum and Instructional Resource Guide* states (page 159): "Because clients with drinking [drug] problems tend to use alcohol [drugs] as a coping strategy and a crisis increases demands on coping, these techniques are important in helping clients stay sober [drug free], learn new coping skills, and solidify their support systems."

Each crisis, as it arises, is a challenge to both the counselor and the client. The challenge to the counselor lies in preempting the power of the crisis as a challenge to the treatment process and thereby reinforcing abstinence as a coping mechanism. The challenge to the client lies in the development of a technique foreign to his/her past experience in times of crisis. The development of the self-denial of the chemical escape in a time of crisis becomes a stepping-stone along the pathway of the new way of life.

In those incidents that require the expertise of other professionals, the counselor should be able to move firmly and quickly to bring them into the picture. Unnecessary delay allows for the client's internal magnification of the situation. The cooperative effort should be done in as calm and professional a manner as circumstances allow. The truly professional counselor will have no reluctance to reach out to others for expertise in recognition of his/her limitations and proper role during emergencies.

The crisis intervention experience should be recorded in sufficient detail to be useful in the future. The progress notes, as discussed in Chapter 6, are of the utmost importance. Adequate counselor's progress notes will provide details and insights for informed revision of the treatment plan by the case management team. Each crisis of reasonable magnitude is an indicator that the treatment plan requires reconsiderations by the team.

Priorities change as the treatment process continues, and the alert counselor will be aware of the sometimes fine nuances in the attitudinal changes in the client. Frequently these *minor* indicators are the forerunner of an acute crisis. The initial period of abstinence while in the treatment system is the formative process in recovery. The counselor who is able to spot an attitude change or loss of attention or focus on the part of the client must not discard or discount it.

© Stanley F. Kulewicz

Terence T. Gorski
1973

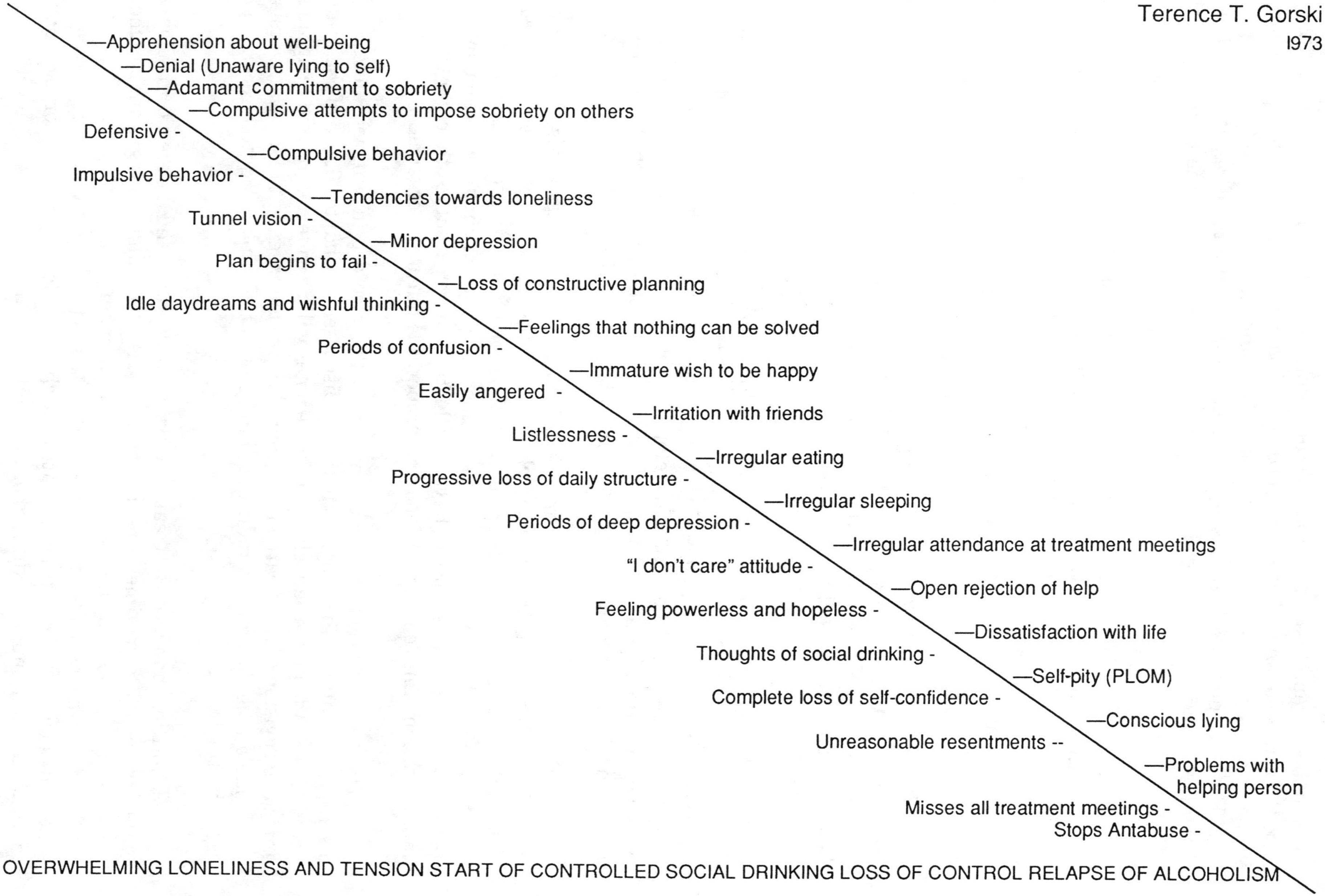

© Stanely F. Kulewicz

9

EDUCATION

EXPANDING THE KNOWLEDGE BASE

The internationally accepted definition of client education is as follows:

"CLIENT EDUCATION—provision of information to individuals and groups, concerning alcohol and other drug abuse and the available services and resources."

The following expanded definition of "education" may be used as a set of general guidelines:

"Client education is provided in a variety of ways. In certain inpatient and residential programs, for example, a sequence of formal classes may be conducted using a didactic format with reading materials and films. On the other hand, an outpatient counselor may provide relevant information to the client individually and informally. In addition to alcohol and drug information, client education may include a description of self-help groups and other resources that are available to the clients and their families."

The education core function has grown in importance to the recovering client in recent years because of the change in educational techniques. The expanded availability of client-directed educational materials has enabled treatment facilities and practitioners to upgrade their educational processes. In the process, many nationally recognized experts have contributed to the education-materials explosion through the expanded use of visual aids, such as videotapes. Facts and figures have been augmented by an enhanced method of delivery of the information to the client. The development of educational personalities, such as Father Martin, Claudia Black and many others, has added a new dimension to the alcohol and drug abuse information transmission system.

The counselor certification applicant is required to be knowledgeable in and demonstrate competency in the core function of client education to the satisfaction of the certifying body.

The counselor, in fulfilling his/her responsibility to the client, must demonstrate an ability to develop an educational program best suited to the individual client. Each client is an individual having capabilities that are different from other clients. Factors such as level of education, reading ability, writing ability, comprehension level, attention span, and previous chemical substance knowledge and understanding must be taken into account when an education program is planned.

 © Stanley F. Kulewicz

The long range effect of a properly organized and effectively presented substance abuse education component cannot be understated. Very often, long after the treatment process has been completed, the chemical substance education serves to counter the environmental pressures to relapse.

In recent years, a wealth of research and scientific study has gone into the subject of addiction to drugs and alcohol, and an extensive library of information now exists. This store of information covers the addiction process in the mind and body as well as the psyche. Current education sources include videotapes, books, cassette tapes, and pamphlets, as well as films.

This vast, newly generated storehouse of knowledge must be utilized with great discretion when introducing it to the newly recovering person. The early introduction of highly technical scientific data could do more harm than good. It is conceivable that a new set of fears and apprehensions may result and have a negative effect in the treatment process. Discretion must be exercised and information must be introduced in a judicious and caring manner. The provision of technical and other pertinent educational materials must be determined by the client's developing capability of comprehending and assimilating heretofore unknown or not understood information.

Basic sources of information lie in the original books and pamphlets from Alcoholics Anonymous World Headquarters in New York City. Though the organization was founded in the interest of arresting the disease of alcoholism, the information is applicable in a unique way to other addictions, with modifications.

For the purposes of this textbook, it must be clearly pointed out that the client education referred to in this core function study is restricted and directed to drug and alcohol addiction and to the resources available for the treatment thereof for clients and their families or significant others.

The education provided to the client and/or significant others may be highly structured, on the one hand, or very informal on the other hand. The circumstances of the treatment setting will be the determining factor.

The PACE curriculum and instructional resource guide list the following areas of counselor knowledge pertinent to the client education process:

"Current statistics on prevalence and incidence of alcohol [drug] abuse."
"Physical, psychological, and social effects of alcohol [drugs]."
"Stages and characteristics of alcoholism [drug addiction]."
"Dynamics of addiction."
"Alcohol/drug interactions; multiple and cross dependence."

Information on self-help groups, or twelve-step programs, falls into the category of information and education, and is generally regarded as basic to the client's addiction education as well as being an informal referral. Among the more prominent of the self-help groups are Alcoholics Anonymous, Narcotics Anonymous, Adult Children of

© Stanley F. Kulewicz

Alcoholics, Alanon, and Alateen.

Family counseling and education techniques usually provide for information on such twelve-step programs, with the recovering client being referred to Alcoholics Anonymous and Narcotics Anonymous. The spouse is generally educated in and referred to the Alanon program, and the teenage offspring are referred to Alateen. Adult offspring are referred to the Adult Children of Alcoholics program.

The last mentioned is the most recently developed self-help twelve- step program of recovery. It has been found to be very useful for those persons who have come from a dysfunctional family as well as alcohol-affected families.

Coordinating the information on self-help groups with the rapidly expanding store of scientific knowledge is an essential component of the treatment process, and the counselor certification applicant can be expected to have to demonstrate competency in this function.

It has been amply demonstrated that the addiction process is being constantly researched, and that scientific study of and the body of knowledge about addiction are expanding continuously. The dedicated counselor will be constantly alert to new information and knowledge to add to his/her inventory of information in order to meet the needs of the client.

 © Stanley F. Kulewicz

10

REFERRAL

REACHING OUT

The internationally accepted definition of referral is as follows:

"Identifying the needs of the client that cannot be met by the counselor or agency and [helping] the client to utilize the support systems and community resources available."

The following supplemental expansion of this definition of "referral" may be used as a set of general guidelines:

"In order to be competent in this function, the counselor must be familiar with community resources, both alcohol / drug and others, and be aware of the limitations of each service. In addition, the counselor must be able to demonstrate a working knowledge of the referral process, including the confidentiality requirements.

"Referral is obviously closely related to case management when integrated into the initial and ongoing treatment plan. It also includes, however, aftercare or discharge planning referrals that take into account the continuum of care."

Each counselor or agency has limited capabilities in the care and treatment of its clients. In general, clients' needs are met by Certified Alcoholism Counselors and Certified Drug Abuse Counselors in conjunction with medical personnel affiliated in the treatment process. Recognition on the part of counselors of their limitations in areas outside of their Substance Abuse Counseling is important. The confidence of the client is enhanced when a counselor recognizes his/her limitations and suggests, to the client, that additional support exists that will help in the resolution of a problem.

If, in the counseling process, indications appear of a possible need for psychiatric or psychological help, a case management session should be held and proper referral made. This action is in the long-range best interests of both the client and the agency.

Dual-diagnosis clients require consultation and referral.

As a result of counseling sessions, ancillary problems may come to light and will need to be addressed. This could require contact outside the initial treatment setting. In this event, the Federal Laws of Confidentiality must be adhered to at all times. A breach of confidentiality is not only an illegal act, it is a violation of the confidence and

© Stanley F. Kulewicz

trust placed in the counselor by the client. A violation of this trust could become very detrimental to the treatment process.

Referral is a means of developing additional components in the developing support system for the client. Those areas that require expertise above and beyond the primary treatment process could be critical to the ongoing abstinence of the client. The cooperative effort resulting from referral and communication with the community support systems will enable the client to expand and maintain a network of support outside the treatment agency. This expanded support will enable the client to grow in his/her abstinence. The correlation and integration of the twelve-core function into a cohesive, comprehensive, and effective treatment process are demonstrated in the direct relationship of the education function to the referral function. In chapter nine, the importance of education in the area of self-help groups in the recovery process was explained. The next obvious step, following education, is the referral to the self-help system of recovery for the development of a new social integration.

The development of the new way of life requires that the client distance him/herself from those environmental influences that could have a negative impact on continued abstinence. In the process of changing, new social contacts and activities are an essential alternative to the previous way of life.

It has been amply demonstrated, for over 50 years, that the recovering addicted person has a far better chance of retaining the state of abstinence through the association with others with like objectives. The most effective nonprofessional support systems that have been developed are the Alcoholics Anonymous and the Narcotics Anonymous twelve-step fellowships.

Informal referral to both on-premises and off-premises self-help groups has been recognized as the most practical and effective ongoing development recommendation.

The counselor certification candidate must demonstrate a recognition of the importance of referral in the long range best interest of the client. The counselor is in an admirable position to recognize needs that can only be met be referral. Special needs identified by the counselor and acted upon through the case management team conference enhance the treatment process.

Referral may be formal, respecting the laws of confidentiality, or it might be an informal referral to a community support system or resource.

Demonstration of a complete working knowledge of the agency's referral process including rules, regulations, laws and protocol is usually required of the substance abuse counselor candidate.

In the event of need to make contact outside the initial serving agency, a *RELEASE / REQUEST OF INFORMATION* form must be obtained from the client. The release, by law, must contain nine points of information. They are listed as follows:

© Stanley F. Kulewicz

1) Client's name
2) Client's date of birth
3) Name and address of program authorized to release information
4) Name and address of recipient of information
5) Specific information to be released
6) Purpose of the release of information
7) Specification of date, event, or condition of expiration
8) Client's signature
9) Date signed by client

Referral, if appropriate, may include state agencies, such as Department of Vocational Education or Department of Income Maintenance, as well as any other relevant resource or service agency, always subject to authorization by the client.

The Discharge Plan may require, for its fulfillment, that contact and information be transferred for the continuation of the treatment process by others outside the initial treatment milieu.

Illustrative forms relevant to confidentiality and disclosure follow this chapter.

 © Stanely F. Kulewicz

PRINCIPLES OF CONFIDENTIALITY FOR ALCOHOL AND DRUG ABUSE TREATMENT RECORDS

1) Federal Regulations take precedence over State Statute unless the latter is stronger.

2) Federal Regulations allow disclosure of patient identifying information only under the following circumstances:

   A) When the patient has consented in writing:

      i) consent must be in the form required by Federal Regulations.
      ii) written notice to the recipient prohibiting redisclosure of the information must accompany the disclosure.

   B) When there is a medical emergency regarding a specific patient.

   C) When a patient commits or threatens to commit a crime on the premises of the program or against program personnel:

      i) report to the police can't identify person as a patient.

   D) To qualified personnel conducting scientific research, management or financial audits, or program evaluation:

      i) redisclosure of patient identifying information by researcher is prohibited.

   E) When it is required by a court order:

      i) a subpoena is not adequate and a hearing must be held before a court order can be issued.
      ii) disclosure is limited to objective data, i.e., dates of enrollment and discharge, attendance, medication, lab reports, etc.

NOTE THAT B, C, D, AND E DO NOT REQUIRE PATIENT CONSENT!

3) If a request for patient identifying information does not fall within the five items listed above,

   i) the information may not be disclosed, and
   ii) your response must be noncommittal. If you are not sure, do not give out any information.

PATIENT IDENTIFYING INFORMATION INCLUDES EVEN THE NAME OF A CURRENT, FORMER, OR DECEASED PATIENT.

 © Stanely F. Kulewicz

CONSENT FOR THE RELEASE OF CONFIDENTIAL INFORMATION

1. I, ____ , AUTHORIZE THE FOLLOWING DISCLOSURE OF INFORMATION FROM MY TREATMENT RECORD:

2. NAME OF PROGRAM THAT IS TO MAKE THE DISCLOSURE:____________
____

3. NAME OR TITLE OF PERSON OR ORGANIZATION TO WHICH THE DISCLOSURE IS TO BE MADE: ______________________________________
____

4. PURPOSE OR NEED OF DISCLOSURE: ______________________________
____

5. EXTENT OR NATURE OF INFORMATION TO BE DISCLOSED: ____________
____

6. DATE OF BIRTH: ____

7. THIS CONSENT IS SUBJECT TO REVOCATION AT ANY TIME EXCEPT TO THE EXTENT THAT ACTION HAS BEEN TAKEN IN RELIANCE THEREON. IF NOT PREVIOUSLY REVOKED, THIS CONSENT WILL TERMINATE UPON (SPECIFIC DATE, EVENT, OR CONDITION):
____

8. SIGNATURE OF PATIENT:____

   SIGNATURE OF PARENT OR GUARDIAN: ___________________________

   SIGNATURE OF PERSON AUTHORIZED TO SIGN IN LIEU OF THE PATIENT (WHERE REQUIRED): ____

9. DATE ON WHICH THIS CONSENT IS SIGNED: _________________________

I understand that my records are protected under the Federal and State confidentiality Regulations and cannot be disclosed without my written consent unless otherwise provided for in the regulations. I also understand that I may revoke this consent at any time except to the extent that action has been taken in reliance on it (e.g., probation or parole) and that in any event this consent expires automatically as described above.

 © Stanely F. Kulewicz

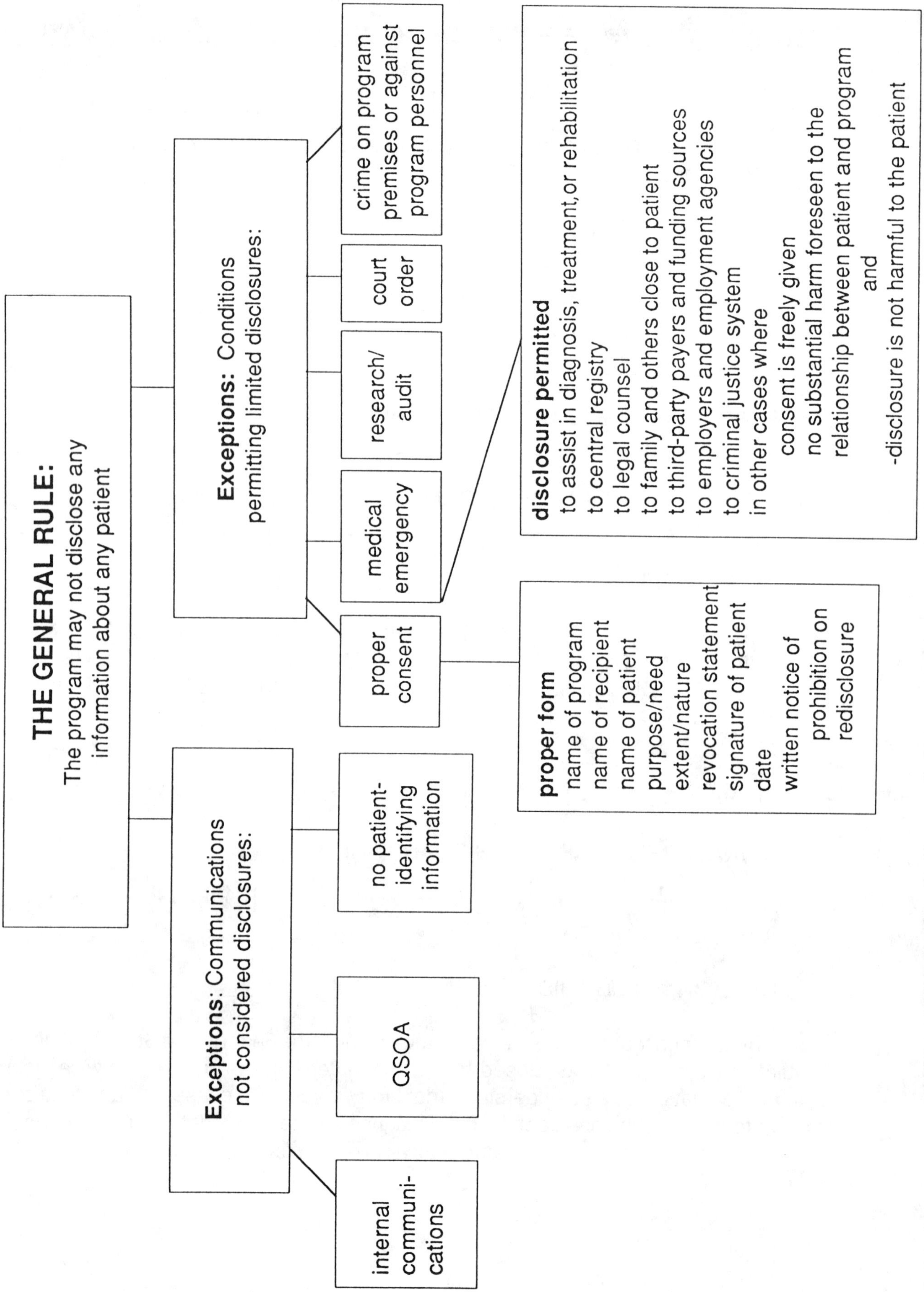

© Stanely F. Kulewicz

11

REPORT AND RECORD KEEPING

HISTORY IN THE MAKING

The internationally accepted definition of report and record keeping is as follows:

"Charting the results of the assessment and treatment plan, and writing reports, progress notes, discharge summaries, and other client-related data."

The following supplemental expanded definition of "report and record keeping" may be used as a set of general guidelines:

"The report and record keeping function is extremely important. It can benefit the counselor by documenting the client's progress in achieving his/her goals. It can facilitate adequate communications between co-workers. It can assist the counselor's supervisor in providing timely feedback. It can be valuable to other programs that may provide services to the client at a later date. It can enhance the accountability of the program to its funding sources. Ultimately, if properly performed, it can enhance the client's treatment experience."

The task that appears to be the least desirable for the counselor is one that is one of the most important in the profession.

The importance of this function in the treatment process cannot be overemphasized. It is a rare counselor who has the ability to reconstruct the counseling history and progress of his/her clients at any given moment without benefit of written progress notes.

Without written progress notes, clinical evaluations and counselor commentaries, the treatment process cannot be regarded as professional behavior. Records and recordkeeping are synonymous with professional standards.

The benefits to the client and the treatment facility of constant, coherent, continuous clinician's progress notes are as follows:

1) Through accurate intake information, written clearly, concisely and completely, the assessment can be properly made.

2) On the basis of the written intake and assessment, a treatment plan can be formulated that would be in the best interest of the client.

© Stanley F. Kulewicz

3) The Case Management team will have accurate records of all that has transpired for the purposes of discussion, consultation, referral, and treatment plan revision.

4) Notes will provide for a continuous pattern of communication on particular subject matters by allowing the counselor to review written notes. The written notes illustrate the pattern of response to counseling. The continuity of the client's perceptions, the history of the varying mood levels, and the emerging new personality are chronologically recorded. Progress toward stated goals will be recorded and progress monitored.

5) Written history of the case will facilitate the change in counselors in the event of need. The loss of a counselor's services through death, illness, vacation, or other reasons makes it imperative that adequate counselor's notes are available to the replacement counselor, in the best interest of the client.

Without proper recordkeeping, the counseling process is haphazard, discontinuous and, ultimately, of limited effectiveness. Inadequate or incomplete clinician's notes do not provide for continuity of care, and the resultant confusion undermines the development of self-discipline on the part of the client. Counselors serve as role models in the early stages of recovery and therefore must demonstrate self-discipline and completeness in this vital area. A counselor who is deficient in proper recordkeeping will reveal his/her lack of self-discipline by consistently demonstrating it through repetitive reviews of past counseling sessions with the client. Though a reasonable amount of review of past counseling sessions is normal and serves a useful purpose, the constant revival of past sessions is not acceptable since it demonstrates a lack of continuity and forward momentum on the part of the counselor.

A periodic review of the counselor's progress notes by the clinical supervisor allows for professional feedback to enhance the counseling process. The additional inquiries, exchange of viewpoints, and discussions with the counselor's record as the information base serve to expand and reinforce the counselor's efforts.

Many agencies are funded by outside sources, and often, the continuation of the funding is dependent upon being able to demonstrate positive results. Without written records giving details of process, technique and results, the validity of the program is in question and funding could be in jeopardy.

Without accurate records denoting unresolved issues, developing problems, or needs for further attention, an adequate discharge plan meeting the client's needs would be almost impossible to formulate, thereby denying the client the full benefit of the treatment program.

The discharge summary should be reasonably brief, but extensive enough to be clear and concise with regard to goal attainment, unresolved issues, recommendations, and referrals.

 © Stanely F. Kulewicz

Referral for further counseling and/or continuing care sometimes requires a counseling history in order that the continuing program is effective. It is in the best interest of the client that this information be available to meet the need of the follow-up counselor or practitioner. Here, as in all other outside contacts, proper release forms must be obtained. It is recommended that notes and records be kept, in reasonable detail, of matters discussed verbally with authorized contacts.

The counselor certification candidate must demonstrate a working knowledge and complete understanding of the importance of adequate report and record keeping as an integral part of the successful counselor's knowledge base. The candidate's competence will be judged on his/her ability to convey recognition of the vital part that records play in the successful completion of the treatment process.

The counselor who has been able to embody the record keeping as an integral part of the core function of assessment will have no trouble in making use of a properly written record. Detailed and continuous clinical notes serve to track the progress of the client and thereby revise the treatment plan on an on-going basis. Periodic review of the client's record provides the counselor with a source of information for use in referral, crisis intervention, education, discharge summary and discharge plan.

Additionally, records serve the agency in accountability for funding and statistical purposes as well as to meet licensing requirements.

Illustrations of a Discharge Plan and a Discharge Summary follow.

© Stanley F. Kulewicz

DISCHARGE SUMMARY

RESIDENT______________________________DATE_______CASE #______

1) Evaluation of progress: Please list each goal identified in the Treatment Plan and provide a brief summary of the progress accomplished.

GOAL PROGRESS

2) Reason for discharge:

3) Summarize course of treatment (problems, experiences, etc.):

4) Recommendations:

5) Referral upon discharge:

© Stanely F. Kulewicz

DISCHARGE PLAN

1) <u>LIVING NEEDS</u>:

A. Where will the resident live after the discharge?______________________

B. Members of the household who will aid the resident with his/her recovery:

____

C. Location within the house where the resident can find peace and quiet:

____

D. Locations, places, persons, and circumstances that the client should avoid:

____

____

E. Other: ____

____

2) <u>VOCATIONAL NEEDS FOR RECOVERY:</u>

A. Employee or self-employed?____________________________________

B. Volunteer work (if so, how will client support him/herself)?_______________

3) <u>SUPPORT SYSTEMS / SELF-HELP GROUPS</u>:

A. Alcoholics Anonymous (AA)____________________________________

B. Narcotics Anonymous (NA) ____________________________________

C. Spiritual support ____

D. Other ____

4) <u>FINANCIAL PLAN FOR SUPPORT</u>:

A. Earnings_______________

B. Relatives_______________

C. Other__________________

5) <u>EDUCATIONAL NEEDS</u>:

A. Educational plans and commitment made toward reaching goals.

____

____

 © Stanely F. Kulewicz

DISCHARGE PLAN

Page 2

6) SUMMARY OF UNRESOLVED PROBLEMS THAT THE CLIENT NEEDS TO ADDRESS ON LEAVING THE TREATMENT CENTER:

____

____

7) FURTHER TREATMENT NEEDS:

A. Outpatient counseling (substance abuse)____________________
B. Psychiatric/psychological counseling____________________
C. Medical____
D. Other____

I agree to the above plan and will carry out those things that are listed above. If I find that I am unable to do this, I will call my counselor and make the necessary changes in the plan that I feel will aid me in refraining from the use of substances.

____________________________ ____________________________

CLIENT COUNSELOR

______________ ______________

DATE DATE

© Stanely F. Kulewicz

12

CONSULTATION WITH OTHER PROFESSIONALS IN REGARD TO CLIENT TREATMENT/SERVICES

WORKING WITH OTHERS

The internationally accepted definition of consultation with other professionals in regard to treatment/services is as follows:

"Relating with our own and other professionals to assure comprehensive, quality care for the client."

The following supplemental expanded definition of "working with others" may be used as a set of general guidelines:

"Consultations are meetings for discussions, decision-making and planning. The most common consultation is the regular in-house staffing in which client cases are reviewed with other members of the treatment team. Consultations also can be conducted in individual sessions with the supervisor, other counselors, psychologists, physicians, probation officers and other service providers connected with the client's case."

The old axiom "no man is an island" fits this last but most certainly not the least of the twelve core functions. Its position as number twelve is designed to reinforce the prior references to working with others. The need for continuing professional knowledge and growth by the counselor can be partially filled by interaction with others in the treatment field. The other professionals in the care of victims of addiction are in a strong position to provide input and information. Their experiences and education, coupled with their contacts with the client, often provide insight and recognitions that the professional counselor can gain from.

The importance of this core function is accented by the type and direction of the inquiries directed to the certification applicant by the examination panel. The focus of the questions is toward specifics of counselor actions in relation to the client. The questioning regarding consultation will require valid explanations of the counseling process itself and the interaction of the counselor and other professionals to meet the needs of the client.

The certification candidate, in demonstrating competence, must indicate an understanding of the need for consultation in areas of expertise that he/she is not experienced in, or has limited expertise in. A willingness to acknowledge the fact that substance abuse counselors are experts in their specific field, but that there are many

© Stanley F. Kulewicz

interrelated circumstances and developments that call for the input of experts in the relevant areas must be demonstrated by the client.

An explanation of the required documentation in the referral process is essential to the demonstration of competence in this core function.

The input from all others involved in the case is essential to the health and well-being of the human being who has come to the facility to save his/her life. At each and every moment in the treatment process, the team must be mindful of the fatality of the disease of Chemical Addiction. The alternative to effective treatment could be death for the client.

Each of the twelve core functions was designed to serve as the guide to provide a comprehensive, cohesive pattern of caring and providing for the needs of the recovering client.

In each and every function, the accent has been to determine that part of the state of being of the client that needs attention in the treatment process. The broad guidelines allow for innovation and flexibility within the overall process of the recovery program. There is recognition of the individual counselor's preference in counseling technique, timing, and his/her personality traits.

The term *treatment process* means just that. It is a process whereby the tools are provided by the counselor to the client to enable the client to heal him/herself. In each developing stage of recovery, new needs are uncovered, old needs are resolved, new issues arise, and old issues are laid to rest. This is a continuing pattern of change. For the addicted person, unfamiliar tools must be introduced to replace the former pattern of chemical escape. The counseling team acts as a conduit to pass on the experiences of the successful to the newcomer.

Without consultation with his/her peers, the counselor is limited by his/her own experience and expertise. In consultation with others, the sharing of experience provides a firmer foundation in the development of strength and hope in the newcomer.

As the treatment process advances and the capabilities of the client increase, there is an increase in recognition of the reality of the past and present as well as a developing concern for the future. The ability to see the possibility of a positive way of life engenders a desire to make improvements in education, occupation, and family relationships. The individual counselor, although exposed to a vast amount of education and training, will recognize his/her limits. Time is one of the major limiting factors.

The primary function of the Substance Abuse Counselor is to help the client develop the coping skills needed to maintain a chemical-free way of life. Peripheral needs must be satisfied through the use of consultations and referrals in the interest of best utilizing the counselor's talents.

The wise counselor is the counselor who recognizes that there are individual

 © Stanley F. Kulewicz

limitations in each counselor and that in concert with other professionals, the maximum benefit can accrue to the client.

In 1939, the book *Alcoholics Anonymous* was published. It is significant to make note of these words written by Bill W., co-founder of Alcoholics Anonymous. His inspired words, written in the formative years of Alcoholics Anonymous, are equally important today to the loving care of the addicted.

"God has abundantly supplied this world with fine doctors, psychologists, and practitioners of various kinds. Do not hesitate to take your health problems to such persons. Most of them give freely of themselves, that their fellows may enjoy sound minds and bodies. Try to remember that though God has wrought miracles among us, we should never belittle a good doctor or psychiatrist. Their services are often indispensable in treating a newcomer and following his case afterward."

 © Stanley F. Kulewicz

REFERENCES

Alcoholics Anonymous (The Big Book), 1939, and "Twelve Steps and Twelve Traditions," 1952, Alcoholics Anonymous World Services, Inc., New York City.

Berne, Eric, M.D. "Games People Play." Grove Press, New York City: 1964.

Egan, Gerard. "The Skilled Helper." Brooks/Cole Publishing Co., Monterey, California: 1975.

Gorski, Terence. "Counseling for Relapse Prevention." Alcoholism Systems Associates, Hazel Crest, Illinois: 1979.

Lair, Jess. "I ain't much, baby—but I'm all I got." Fawcett Publications, Greenwich, Connecticut: 1969.

International Certification Reciprocity Consortium/Alcohol and Other Drug Abuse, Inc. "Case Presentation Method Trainer's Manual." ICRC/AODA, Inc., Atkinson, New Hampshire: 1986.

Rodgers, C.R., and Truax, C.B. "The Therapeutic Relationship and Its Impact." University of Wisconsin Press: 1967.

U.S. Department of Health and Human Services. "Planning Alcoholism Counseling Education (PACE)": 1982.

Wallace, John. "Alcoholism: New Light on the Disease." Edgehill Publications, Newport, Rhode Island: 1985.

 © Stanely F. Kulewicz

ACKNOWLEDGMENTS

The author extends his heartfelt thanks to the many persons who provided encouragement and support in the compilation of this textbook.

Special thanks to the following organizations, which generously provided forms and permission to use them in this effort to provide a comprehensive basic text on the core functions of counselors:

A.D.R.C., Inc., Hartford, Connecticut

Connecticut Alcohol and Drug Abuse Commission (CADAC)

Dixwell Opposes Alcoholism (DOA), New Haven, Connecticut

McCall Foundation, Torrington, Connecticut

Northeast Connecticut Alcohol Council, Willimantic, Connecticut

Stonington Institute, North Stonington, Connecticut

A very special thanks to the Connecticut Alcoholism and Drug Abuse Counselor Certification Board, Inc., and Maureen Mullane, without whose help nothing could have come about.

 © Stanely F. Kulewicz

NOTES

NOTES

© Stanely F. Kulewic

NOTES

NOTES

NOTES

© Stanely F. Kulewic